Joseph's Dilemma

Joseph's Dilemma

"Honor Killing" in the Birth Narrative of Matthew

MATTHEW J. MAROHL

CASCADE *Books* · Eugene, Oregon

JOSEPH'S DILEMMA:
"Honor Killing" in the Birth Narrative of Matthew

Cascade Books
A Division of Wipf and Stock Publishers
199 W. 8th Ave., Suite 3
Eugene, OR 97401

www.wipfandstock.com

ISBN 13: 978-1-55635-825-8

Cataloging-in-Publication data:

Marohl, Matthew J.

Joseph's dilemma : "honor killing" in the birth narrative of Matthew / Matthew J. Marohl.

xviii + 86 p. ; 23 cm. — Includes bibliographical references.

ISBN 13: 978-1-55635-825-8

1. Bible N. T. Matthew—Criticism, interpretation, etc. 2. Honor in the Bible. 3. Shame in the Bible. 4. Honor Killings. 5. Joseph, Saint. I. Title

BS2458. M1 2008

Manufactured in the U.S.A.

To my wife, Sarah

and

To my daughter, Noa

Contents

Acknowledgements

Thank you to Dr. Chris Spinks at Wipf and Stock Publishers for support-
ing this project and for help and advice in the final stages of preparing the
manuscript for publication. Thank you to Rev. Dr. Ritva Williams and to
The Context Group for your critical reading of the first two chapters of
this book. Your expertise on the cultural values of honor and shame are
invaluable. Thank you to Rev. Brant A.B. Clements for both your theological insights and your editing skills. Thank you to Dr. Emil Kramer for your
extensive knowledge of classical literature, but more importantly for your
friendship. Finally, thank you to all of the women and men who fight on
behalf of human rights around the world. All remaining inaccuracies and
errors are my responsibility.

Matthew J. Marohl

May, 2008

Introduction

STORIES OF THE REALITY AND brutality of honor killings come from many sources. Newspapers and magazines around the world tell of the killing of women by shamed family members, killings meant to restore family honor.[1] A wide variety of books explore the lives of women who live with the reality of such violence.[2] Documentary films offer a personal glimpse into the lives of men and women affected by the crime.[3] And when we listen closely, the words of musicians, artists, and poets tell the story of women wiped out in blood. Nazik al-Malaika, an Iraqi feminist poet, tells the story of murder in the name of family honor.

> Dawn will come and the girls will ask about her,
> Where is she? And the monster will answer:
> "We killed her."
> A mark of shame was on our forehead and we washed it off.
>
> Her black tale will be told by neighbours,
> And will be told in the quarter even by the palm trees,
> Even the wooden doors will not forget her,
> It will be whispered even by the stones.
> Washing off the shame . . . Washing off the shame.
> O neighbours, O village girls,
> Bread we shall knead with our tears.

1. Many examples will be provided in chapter 1. However, for a helpful introduction, see Ruggi, "Honor Killing in Palestine," 12–15.

2. For an example that follows the lives of women in Iraq from birth to old age, see al-Khayyat, *Honour and Shame*.

3. For two recent examples, see *In the Morning* and *Love, Honor, & Disobey*.

We'll shear our plaits and skin our hands,
To keep their clothes white and pure,
No smile, no joy, no turn as the knife so waiting
For us in the hand of father or brother
And tomorrow, who knows which desert
Swallows us, to wash off shame?[4]

It is in this context, the context of honor killings, the context of family honor and family shame that we must hear the birth narrative in Matthew. The story is told in eight verses and embedded in this short account is "Joseph's dilemma." Listeners are told that, "When Mary had been engaged to Joseph, but before they lived together, she was found to be with child from the Holy Spirit" (1:18). What happens next has long been debated. We are made to assume that Joseph discovers that Mary is pregnant, but not that she is with child from the Holy Spirit. This information is made known to Joseph later by an angel of the Lord who appeared to him in a dream. In the meantime, Joseph must decide what he will do with Mary.

We are told that "Joseph, being a righteous man and unwilling to expose her to public disgrace, planned to dismiss her quietly" (1:19). The discussion of this verse generally focuses on two questions. First, did Joseph suspect Mary of adultery? Second, if he did suspect Mary of adultery, what where his options? While there is some diversity in the way these questions are answered, the majority of modern interpreters envision only one option—that of divorce. The dilemma, then, is whether Joseph will divorce Mary "publicly" or "privately." While this discussion reflects the view of the majority, it does not adequately address Joseph's dilemma. In this book, I will argue that early Christ-followers understood Joseph's dilemma to involve an assumption of adultery and the subsequent possibility of killing Mary. Worded differently, Joseph's dilemma involves the possibility of an honor killing. If Joseph reveals that Mary is pregnant she might be killed. If Joseph conceals Mary's pregnancy, he will be opposing the law of the Lord. What is a "righteous" man to do?

For some, this thesis may be difficult to accept. In fact, it may sound heretical to argue that Joseph's dilemma involves the possible murder of Mary (and, therefore, the killing of Jesus). I will argue, however, that this reading actually introduces an important Matthean theme—*from expected*

---

4. al-Khayyat, *Honour and Shame*, 35–36. This poem was originally written in Arabic and was translated into English by al-Khayyat. The original Arabic citation is from al-Malaika, *A Tranquil Moment of a Wave*.

death comes unexpected new life. This theme runs throughout the gospel and culminates in the death and resurrection of Jesus. Therefore, while the majority of this book will focus on a single story, the interpretation of Joseph's dilemma will inform my reading of Matthew as a whole.

The structure for this work is quite simple. I will begin by providing a thorough description of modern honor killings. While the consideration of the cultural values of honor and shame has become commonplace in the study of the New Testament world, I am not aware of a single, detailed analysis of honor killings by a biblical interpreter.[5] In fact, many (perhaps most) biblical interpreters do not discuss the possible killing of Mary.[6] For those that do acknowledge that the "law commands severe penalties," the killing of Mary is only hinted at and the reality of an honor killing is left unaddressed. Robert H. Smith provides a helpful example of the vague nature of such an interpretation of Matt 1:19:

> The Law commanded severe penalties for sexual sins (Deut. 22:13-27). Matthew does not indulge in speculation about the hurt feelings of Joseph or tortured disclaimers of Mary but focuses entirely on the character of Joseph as **a just man** (*dikaios*, cf. 13:43, 49; 25:37, 46; 27:4, 19, 24), a man of righteousness, a quality lifted up and celebrated in the Gospel more than in any of the others . . . As a man of righteousness, Joseph planned to follow the old law and put Mary aside. But mercy struggled in Joseph with his sense of right, and he resolved to divorce her **quietly** without exposing her to public shame.[7]

While Smith notes that the "law commanded severe penalties for sexual sins," he does not make explicit the nature of the penalties. This vague interpretation of Matt 1:19 is further complicated as he juxtaposes "putting Mary aside" with "divorcing her quietly." Quite simply, it is not clear what

---

5. A search of New Testament Abstracts does not reveal a single use of the term, "honor killing." Furthermore, a search of the ATLA Religion Database does not reveal a single use of the term by a biblical interpreter. In short, biblical interpreters do not appear to have considered the possibility that an honor killing serves as the context for Matthew's birth narrative.

6. In chapter 2, I will provide a detailed examination of various interpretations of Matt 1:19. For an example of an interpretation that considers the cultural values of honor and shame, but lacks a discussion of honor killings, see Malina and Rohrbaugh, *Social-Science Commentary on the Synoptic Gospels*, 26.

7. Smith, *Matthew*, 35–36.

Smith is alluding to in his description of Joseph's dilemma. It is clear, however, that he does not include a discussion of honor killings.

There are likely many reasons for vagueness—even silence—when discussing Joseph's dilemma. The reason most often implied in North Atlantic biblical interpretation is lack of awareness of the *reality* of honor killings. A small number of interpreters mention the threat of death for Mary. Unfortunately, it is commonly viewed as *only a threat*. For many, it is believed that honor killings "never really occurred."[8] For this reason, I will begin by outlining the modern practice of honor killings. If we become aware of this very real violent crime, new questions will necessarily arise. If this practice occurs today, did it occur in the first century? If so, how might early Christ-followers have understood the birth story in Matthew's gospel? How might this inform our reading of the text?

After my description of modern honor killings, I will outline various modern interpretations of the birth story in Matthew. Two topics will dominate this discussion. Did Joseph suspect Mary of adultery? If so, what were Joseph's options for punishment? It is here that we are made aware of the silence regarding honor killings. Joseph's dilemma is acknowledged, but the descriptions of his options for punishment reveal two fundamental problems. First, modern biblical interpreters emphasize the need to defend the honor of Mary, rather than the honor of the family. Second, interpreters commonly envision only one option for punishment, that of divorce.

Did honor killings actually occur in the New Testament world? This question is the single focus of chapter 3. After examining a wide body of evidence, a positive answer to the question emerges. However, we will find that just as modern honor killings are often kept silent, the same was true in the first century. While not speaking of adultery, Josephus reveals in vivid detail the relationship between silence and sexual violence. He explains that as the Judean delegates recalled Herod's misrule, they told of the rape and subsequent silence that often accompanied the collecting of taxes:

---

8. The belief that honor killings did not occur in the first century is common and will be discussed in detail in the second chapter. For an example, see Beare, *The Gospel According to Matthew*, 68. Beare writes, "There is no evidence that this penalty was imposed at the time of the Gospel, but a public repudiation would certainly bring lasting shame upon the woman." Similarly, Ulrich Luz writes, "According to Deut 22:23–24 the punishment required for adultery in the case of betrothed persons is stoning. Admittedly, it was no longer practiced in that day." Luz, *Matthew 1–7*, 94.

> In addition to the collecting of the tribute that was imposed on
> everyone each year, lavish extra contributions had to be made to
> [Herod] and his household and friends and those of his slaves who
> were sent out to collect the tribute because there was no immunity
> at all from outrage unless bribes were paid. Moreover, about the
> corrupting of their virgin daughters, and the debauching of their
> wives, victims of drunken violence and bestiality, they were silent
> only because those who suffer such indignities are just as pleased
> to have them remain undisclosed as they are not to have had them
> happen at all.[9]

In short, while there is evidence of honor killings in the New Testament
world, it seems clear that the stories of many victims were never written
down or passed along.

After concluding that honor killings did occur in the first century and
that Joseph's dilemma involved the possible honor killing of Mary, I will argue that this theme establishes a narrative pattern that is visible throughout
the gospel. The author of Matthew continually emphasizes that from expected death comes unexpected new life. Jesus might have been killed before he was even born, but the unexpected occurred and new life emerged.
Jesus might have been killed before his second birthday, but through the
flight to Egypt, new life emerged. This pattern continues throughout the life
of Jesus. Furthermore, while both examples above are literal movements
from expected death to unexpected new life, the author of Matthew also
presents this theme as a metaphor. Finally, Matthew emphasizes that this
pattern is replicated time and time again in the lives of Jesus' followers.
There is, then, good news embedded in Joseph's dilemma.

Before I begin, it is essential to acknowledge an important warning regarding the discussion of honor killings. Instructors of Middle East Studies
commonly emphasize a tendency among many Western (or North Atlantic)
individuals: whether intentional or not, the discussion of honor killings
is often neocolonialist in nature. An examination of what "they" do may
have the effect of perpetuating the stereotype that Middle Eastern societies
are/were "backwards." Furthermore, such representations may perpetuate
"first-world/third-world" hierarchies. In this book, I will attempt to join a
host of Middle Eastern voices and write against the grain of such neocolonialist tendencies.

9. Josephus, *Ant.* 17.308–9.

In her discussion of honor killings, Nadine Naber explains ". . . teaching against the grain of neocolonialist first-world/third-world hierarchies has become a central component of Middle East Studies . . . ."[10] While there are various ways to write against the grain of neocolonialism, many anthropologists seek to contextualize the issue of honor killings in terms of human rights. In other words, honor killings may be understood as one way, among many, that men control or oppress women throughout the world. Everyone, then, is forced to consider the oppression of women present in their own societies. Naber explains how Americans may wish to use comparison as a strategy for teaching.

> . . . teaching against the grain of US media images of Middle Eastern women's supra-oppression, might entail: exploring the ways that rape in the US is institutionalized and protected by religion, universities, and the police force; quoting a US census statistic that shows that in 1991, in the US, 171,420 rapes were reported and that 2.3 million female rapes were reported between 1973 and 1987; teaching about how the historical concept (8th century) that wives are the property of their husbands continues to shape laws about rape and spousal abuse in the US; and looking at the north American states where women are not totally protected from rape by their husbands and where numerous women have been executed or imprisoned for killing their husbands out of self-defense.[11]

In other words, comparing the violence that is deeply embedded in our own culture with the violence of honor killings may help to reduce our neocolonialist tendencies.

A second strategy for writing against the grain of neocolonialism is to include examples of resistance. Naber explains, "I argued for demystifying images of supra-oppressed Middle Eastern women by teaching about Middle Eastern women's resistance, such as the thousand Jordanian women who marched in the streets after a recent honor killing."[12] Similarly, al-Fanar, a Palestinian feminist organization, emphasizes resistance to crimes of honor. A 1995 al-Fanar report offered several examples of demonstrations against honor crimes and provided a brief history of the organization's involvement with such demonstrations:

10. Naber, "Teaching About Honor Killings," 20.

11. Ibid.

12. Ibid., 21.

Introduction

> The first [al-Fanar] demonstration on this issue took place in June 1991, protesting the murder of a 19 year-old pregnant woman by her father and brother (it was later found that she had been raped by a family member). Political organizations, women's organizations in Palestinian society and Israeli women's organizations were invited to join the demonstration. Except for the members and supports of al-Fanar, not one representative of any other political or women's organization took part. The fear was immense. A leader of a Palestinian women's organization claimed that she could not participate in the demonstration because her presence could be construed as being "support for the girl's immoral behavior." The social taboo surrounding this issue and the lack of public acknowledgement was so great that even women who were personally angry about the phenomenon, feared social ostracizing or gossip. In contrast, Israeli feminists claimed that they could not understand what was the murder of women against the background of "family honor". In the course of 3.5 years of the organizations existence, al-Fanar held six demonstrations against murders and attempted murders of women. All earned media coverage which fueled the public debate. It appears that the phenomenon of ignorance and the taboo have disappeared, and that the walls of silence have been brought down. Today this struggle is gaining numerous supporters and sympathizers.[13]

While al-Fanar may be overestimating their own success (e.g., it is unlikely that the "phenomenon of ignorance and the taboo have disappeared" or that "the walls of silence have been brought down"), they do identify a growing public resistance to honor killings. Awareness of such demonstrations may show the complexity of the discussion of honor killings and again help to fight against neocolonialism. It is, then, with both enthusiasm and caution that I invite you to rethink Joseph's dilemma.

13. Al-Fanar, *Developments in the Struggle against the Murder of Women*, 41.

1

The Modern Practice
of Honor Killings

THE TOPIC OF HONOR KILLINGS, whether modern or ancient, is difficult. I choose the word "difficult" carefully and for a variety of reasons. It is, of course, difficult to consider that girls and women throughout the world suffer death at the hands of boys and men. It is also difficult, as noted in the introduction, to discuss honor killings without developing a sense of cultural superiority, without developing a sense of "us" and "them." We may be tempted to think that *we* are not capable of such violent crimes. However, the discussion of honor killings is difficult for yet another reason. Namely, we are presented with difficult challenges regarding *evidence*. That is not to say that there is not evidence. It is clear that honor killings happen at alarming rates. It is to say, however, that the evidence may not always come from typical "academic" sources.[1] Therefore, when it comes to the discussion of honor killings, we have a good deal of evidence at one level (e.g., ethnographies, magazines, and newspapers)[2] and little evidence

1. Biblical interpreters have a long history of using a wide variety of sources. For example, ancient graffiti, coins, and pottery all reveal a great deal about the social world of the Mediterranean region.

2. I have included many 2006 and 2007 newspaper articles in my bibliography. Please note the extent to which honor killings are part of our current discussion of world news

at another (e.g., government statistics, legal rulings, and scholarly journal articles).[3] Our introduction to modern honor killings, then, includes many voices. We will not only hear from experts in Mediterranean and Middle East Studies, but we will also hear from a variety of women and men whose lives have been forever changed by honor killings.

Honor and Shame: A Brief Introduction[4]

The discussion of modern honor killings in the Mediterranean world is necessarily part of a larger discussion of the core cultural values of honor and shame. To begin, one's honor represents the value of a person in his or her own eyes, but also in the eyes of his or her society. In other words, honor is a social value. It is not determined by the "self," but must be recognized by others.[5] There are two ways in which individuals receive honor. First, honor is *ascribed*. This is the honor status that one receives at birth (e.g., you receive the honor status of your family, of your town, etc.). Second, honor is *acquired*. Since honor is considered limited, or finite, it may be challenged through a variety of social interactions. Through public challenges and responses, honor is either protected or lost. All the while, this remains a social activity. In other words, the social group determines the victor and the loser in an honor challenge.[6]

While ascribed honor is certainly important for understanding this complex social system, it is acquired honor that we must more fully explore in our discussion of honor killings. In Mediterranean societies, nearly every

---

and human rights. It is also worth noting that most of the articles were published in Australia and the United Kingdom, with very few published in the United States.

3. For a recent (2006) study of honor killings, see Parrot and Cummings, *Forsaken Females*, 173–87.

4. This introduction to the cultural values of honor and shame is by design, very brief. However, honor and shame in the Mediterranean world have been studied extensively over the past fifty years. For early (and now classic) examples, see Peristiany, *Honour and Shame*, 21–77; or Pitt-Rivers, *The Fate of Shechem*, 1–17. For recent examples, see Horden and Purcell, *The Corrupting Sea*, 485–523; or Barton, *Roman Honor*, 34–87. For examples from biblical interpreters, see Malina, *The New Testament World*, 27–57; or Moxnes, "Honor and Shame," 19–40.

5. Peristiany, *Honour and Shame*, 21. See also, Moxnes, "Honor and Shame," 20.

6. Ibid., 23–35. See also, Moxnes, "Honor and Shame," 20–21.

social interaction is considered a competition for honor recognition.[7] Even the smallest of actions may be considered a challenge to one's honor. For example, asking a question in public may be an honor challenge. Is the answer known? How will others view the exchange? Such interactions take the form of a challenge and a riposte. While most challenges are verbal, they may also be physical or in the form of a gesture or a look. Furthermore, only social equals (or near social equals) may compete for honor.[8] In short, the interplay between challenge and riposte functions as a social contest. After exchanges have been made, the spectators determine the winner. In this case, the winner has successfully defended his honor (or successfully challenged the honor of another), while the loser has been publicly shamed.

Finally, it is very important to acknowledge the role of collective honor, or family honor.[9] Mediterranean societies tend to emphasize collective honor (e.g., the honor of the family) over individual honor.[10] In other words, Mediterranean people tend to understand themselves as being embedded in a family. Furthermore, the family is the primary social unit, not the individual. Therefore, it is the family and its collective honor that is at stake in an honor challenge. As we will see below, in the case of an honor killing, it is the honor of the entire family that is at stake when a female is perceived to have engaged in improper sexual behavior. The actions of the male(s), then, are thought to restore collective honor, the honor status of the family.

---

7. Esler, *The First Christians in their Social Worlds*, 27. Esler notes that, "Virtually any form of social intercourse—gift-giving, dinner invitations, discussions in public places, buying and selling, arranging marriages and any form of agreements on matters of common interest—opens up the participants an opportunity to enhance one's honour at the expense of someone else."

8. Peristiany, *Honour and Shame*, 31. See also, Moxnes, "Honor and Shame," 20.

9. For a discussion of social groups and collective honor, see ibid., 35–39.

10. The discussion of individual and collective honor is part of the larger discussion of "individualism" and "collectivism." Both cultural anthropologists and cross-cultural social psychologists describe cultures in terms of their relative individualist or collectivist tendencies. While cultures which are more individualistic in nature tend to emphasize the individual and the immediate family, cultures that are more collectivist emphasize commitment to a highly organized, hierarchical, and interdependent ingroup. America is commonly described as being very individualistic. In contrast, Middle Eastern and Mediterranean societies tend to be quite collectivist. For examples of relevant research, see Marohl, *Faithfulness and the Purpose of Hebrews*, 85–89; or Triandis, "Cross-Cultural Studies in Individualism and Collectivism," 41–133.

It is here that some readers may raise objections. Is there really such a unity within the Mediterranean world regarding honor and shame? Are there differences between rural and urban social groups? Do other factors such as income or religion inform an individual's understanding of honor and shame? While it is impossible to completely address the complex nature of honor and shame within the diversity of the Mediterranean, it is possible to provide a preliminary answer. Stanley Brandes explains that a unity does exist between the beliefs and attitudes of the many people in this small, but highly diverse, part of the world.

> For one thing, honor—which might best be translated as esteem, respect, prestige, or some combination of these attributes, depending on local usages—is treated throughout the area as a sort of limited good, in George Foster's sense (1965). Wherever we look, Mediterranean honor appears to be related to control over scarce resources, including of course, land and property, political power, and perhaps most notably, female sexuality, with its procreative potential.[11]

Importantly, Brandes highlights the interrelationship between the concept of honor and its social function. In this case, honor is related to control over resources. While many limited resources are controlled through honor contests, the control of female sexuality is emphasized. Similarly, Kitty Warnock explains that a comparison between women throughout the Middle East is possible. She notes, "The lives of women, both Muslim and Christian, were framed in a similar ideology of family, honour and chastity."[12] It is, again, the interrelationship between family, honor, and chastity that will dominate our discussion of honor killings.

So what, then, does this all mean? In short, to understand modern honor killings we must be keenly aware of two central issues. First, we must understand the nature of honor and shame. In particular, we must understand the exchange of challenge and riposte for acquired honor. Second, we must understand that Mediterranean societies place great importance on collective honor, or family honor. When the honor of the family is challenged, the males must respond. When a female member of the family is understood to have threatened the family's honor with the perceived misuse of her sexuality, the males must respond.

11. Brandes, "Reflections on Honor and Shame in the Mediterranean," 121–22.
12. Warnock, *Land Before Honour*, 19.

What Is an Honor Killing?[13]

Honor killing is the practice of killing girls and women who are thought to have endangered a family's honor by allegedly engaging in sexual activity before (or outside of) marriage.[14] Suzanne Ruggi, a staff reporter for *The Jerusalem Times* offers a concise introduction to the discussion of honor killings. Ruggi explains, "[T]he family constitutes the fundamental building block of Palestinian society. Family status is largely dependent upon its honor, much of which is determined by the respectability of its daughters, who can damage it irreparably by the perceived misuse of their sexuality."[15] In the case of such irreparable damage, the males of the family may punish the girl with death. Sana al-Khayyat explains, "A girl who loses her virginity is liable to be punished with physical or 'moral' death; the latter involves isolation and virtual house arrest."[16] The former, of course, is the very real killing of the girl.

While the definition above focuses on a girl's loss of virginity, this is not the only sexual activity that might be punishable by death. Honor killings are also executed in instances of rape, child sexual abuse, and even perceived flirting. Moreover, mere allegations of improper behavior on the part of a girl or woman are often enough to defile a family's honor and "warrant" an honor killing.[17] Alessandra Antonelli tells the story of Aida. Aida was raped at the age of fifteen and was married at twenty. Aida was killed two days after her wedding. A girl from the village of al-Jalil in Palestine, she was molested by her uncle when she was a teenager. Her family knew of the molestation. When her husband brought her back complaining that the girl was not a virgin, Aida's own father killed her.[18]

It is after the telling of Aida's story that Antonelli emphasizes that honor killings must be understood as violent crimes. She quotes Suad Abu Daya, head of the social workers' unit at the Women's Center for Legal Aid and Counseling in Jerusalem, "These are crimes not stories. It is too simple

---

13. For a textbook definition, see Burn, *Women Across Cultures*, 30.

14. Newell et al., *Discrimination Against the Girl Child*, 18.

15. Ruggi, *Honor Killings in Palestine*, 13.

16. al-Khayyat, *Honour and Shame*, 34.

17. Newell et al., *Discrimination Against the Girl Child*, 18.

18. Antonelli, "Crimes not Stories," 13. Antonelli notes that Aida's name was changed in her telling of the story.

to call them honor killings—these are woman killings."[19] Similarly, The Palestinian Human Rights Monitoring Group explains, "Killing women on the basis of family honor is considered one of the forms of discrimination against woman [sic] and is a serious violation of her basic human rights."[20] The Youth Advocate Program International, Katherine S. Newell, and others also place the discussion of honor killings into the broader arena of abuse and human rights.[21] In short, it is not sufficient to describe honor killings solely in terms of the complex code of honor and shame, honor killings must also be understood to be violent crimes and human rights violations.

Where do honor killings occur?[22] In their discussion of the crime, Newell and her co-authors, highlight the countries in which honor killings are most widely reported: "Honor killing is an extreme form of child abuse and domestic violence. While child abuse and domestic violence are present in virtually every part of the world and may result in death, the tradition of honor killing is most widely reported in Egypt, India, Iran, Iraq, Israel (among Arab Israelis), Jordan, Lebanon, Pakistan, Palestine, Syria, Turkey, and Yemen."[23] The practice of honor killings also occurs in countries outside of the Middle East.[24] For example, the United Kingdom has experienced an increase in honor killings by Middle Eastern refugees and immigrants.[25]

Everyone who discusses honor killings acknowledges that it is impossible to know the actual number of girls and women killed each year.[26] Suzanne Ruggi explains, "Given that honor killings often remain a private family affair, no official statistics are available on the practice or its

19. Antonelli, "Crimes not Stories," 13.

20. Palestinian Human Rights Monitoring Group, "Honor Killing," 4.

21. Newell et al., *Discrimination Against the Girl Child*, 18.

22. Andrea Parrot and Nina Cummings note that honor killings occur in Afghanistan, Bangladesh, China, Egypt, Great Britain, Ecuador, India, Iran, Iraq, Israel, Italy, Jordan, Korea, Lebanon, Pakistan, Palestine, Morocco, Sweden, Syria, Turkey, Uganda, and Yemen. They also explain that in Latin America such murders are called "crimes of passion." Parrot and Cummings, *Forsaken Females*, 173.

23. Newell et al., *Discrimination Against the Girl Child*, 18.

24. For a recent discussion of migration and honor killings, see Parrot and Cummings, *Forsaken Females*, 182.

25. Smith, "Muslim killed daughter for the 'dishonour' of having boyfriend," 5.

26. The United Nations estimates that more than five thousand women worldwide are killed each year in the name of family honor. Parrot and Cummings, *Forsaken Females*, 173.

frequency."[27] Likewise, Newell and others note that "it is believed that hundreds of girls and women are killed each year in the name of honor, but the true scope of the problem is still largely unknown."[28] Newell and her colleagues do offer rough statistics for the period of 1997–99. Although these numbers are already a decade old, they remain a helpful introduction to the scope of honor killings.

> In Pakistan in 1999, 364 girls and women were reported victims of honor killings in the Sindh province alone. In Jordan in 1998, there were 20 reported honor killings. In Egypt in 1997, there were 52 honor killings out of 843 premeditated murders. In Lebanon there were 36 reported honor killings between 1996 and 1998. In Israel, the West Bank, and the Gaza Strip there were 64 reported honor crimes between 1990 and 1999. However, a women's organization working with the Gaza Strip believes that between the years of 1996 and 1998, 177 cases reported as natural deaths in the Gaza Strip were actually honor killings. In Yemen surveys completed by Mohammed Ba Obaid, head of the Women's Studies department of Sanaa University, found more than 400 women were reported victims of honor killings in 1997, the last year for which research is complete.[29]

While these numbers are disturbingly high, there is actually indication that honor killings are increasing in some areas.[30] According to a 2007 report prepared by Ohaila Shomar coordinator of SAWA (All Women Together Today and Tomorrow) which operates a hotline for battered Palestinian women, violence against women in Palestine is on the rise. Khaled Abu Toameh, reporting for *The Jerusalem Post* explains the report.

> The report which was a group effort between SAWA and other organizations showed that at least 48 women have been killed in the last three years in the West Bank and the Gaza Strip as a result of domestic violence. Until 2004, the number of Palestinian women murdered every year ranged between 10 and 12. Most victims were murdered for allegedly bringing "shame" on male members of their

27. Ruggi, *Honor Killings in Palestine*, 12.

28. Newell et al., *Discriminating Against the Girl Child*, 19.

29. Ibid.

30. See also Jaber, "'Honour' Killings Grow as Girl, 17, Stoned to Death," 25; Loudon, "Pakistan Police Fail as 'Honour Killings Soar,'" 16; and Nickerson, "For Muslim Women, A Deadly Defiance: 'Honor Killings' on Rise in Europe," A1.

families. The victims' ages ranged between 12 and 85. Shomar who for years has helped Palestinian women deal with violence and sexual abuse said that 32 of the cases where related to "honor killings" and all except two of the victims were Muslims.[31]

The report pointed out that the "real problem was the absence of a proper law to punish the perpetrators. The Palestinians still use a Jordanian law dating back to 1960 which imposes a light sentence on men involved in honor killings."[32] The light sentencing of men involved in honor killings is echoed by many in the discussion of honor killings. In 2003, Mark Franchetti, a reporter for *The Sunday Times* (London), also emphasized an increase in honor killings in Iraq and the light sentences for men involved in the crime. Franchetti explains that honor killings "have increased sharply amid the breakdown in security that has blighted Iraq since the fall of Saddam Hussein."[33] Furthermore, if an Iraqi male is found guilty of committing an honor killing, the maximum sentence is one year in prison.

Descriptions of Honor Killings in Narrative Form

In the previous section, I provided an "encyclopedia-style" description of honor killings. It does not take long, however, before one realizes that honor killings are not always described in such formal language.[34] In fact, it is often through very personal narratives that women and men share their experiences with this violent crime. Lama Abu-Odeh answers the question, "What is a crime of honor?" with a graphic story that invites readers into the world of honor killings.

> "Where were you, bitch?" Maria Isa snapped as her daughter, Tina, 16, entered the family apartment.
> "Working," Tina shot back.
> "We do not accept that you go to work," interrupted Tina's father, Zein.
> "Why are you doing this to us?" asked Maria angrily.
> "I am not doing anything to you," Tina bristled.

31. Abu-Toameh, "Report says Palestinian 'honor killings' are increasing," 3.

32. Ibid.

33. Franchetti, "Iraqi women die in 'honour' murders," 25.

34. For a recent (2007) example of an historical fictional narrative of an honor killing, see Tintori, *Unto the Daughters*.

"You are a she-devil," hissed Zein, "and what about the boy who walked you home? He wants to sleep with you in bed, don't you have any shame? Don't you have a conscience? It's fornication."

With that her parents threatened to throw Tina out of the apartment; rebelliously she challenged them to do it.

"Listen, my dear daughter," her father finally replied, "do you know that this is the last day? Tonight you're going to die?"

"Huh?" said Tina bewildered.

"Do you know that you are going to die tonight?"

Suddenly, realising he was serious, Tina let out a long scream. Then there was a crash, and the girl's shrieks became muffled, as if someone were trying to cover her mouth.

"Keep still, Tina," her father shouted.

"Mother, please help me," Tina cried.

But her mother would not help. Instead, she held her struggling daughter down as Zein began stabbing Tina in the chest with a seven inch boning knife.

"No, please!" Tina cried.

"Shut up!" Her mother shouted.

"No! No!" Tina shrieked.

"Die! Die quickly! Die quickly!" Her father shouted.

Tina managed to scream again.

"Quiet, little one," her father said, stabbing her the last six times. "Die, my daughter, die!"[35]

For Abu-Odeh, this narrative functions as a definition of a "crime of honor," but it also invites the reader to glimpse the emotion and violence of the crime.

Similarly, Souad, a resident of a small village in the West Bank, tells of her escape from an honor killing in narrative form. Souad had an affair with a young man before marriage and became pregnant. While she loved the boy and believed that they would be together, he abandoned her shortly after she became pregnant. When her pregnancy was discovered by her family, it was decided that she must be killed. She describes the practice: "If you don't kill a girl who has dishonoured her family, villagers will reject the family, and nobody will speak to them or do business with them. They have to leave."[36] Her family, therefore, felt forced to defend its honor and to restore its public standing. As Souad worked in the yard, gasoline was poured

35. Abu-Odeh, *Crimes of Honor*, 142–143.
36. Souad, *Burned Alive*, 27.

over her head and she was set on fire. Remarkably, Souad survived the attempted honor killing. In the hospital, she reasoned, "My mother was an excellent mother, the best of mothers, she was doing her duty in giving me death. It was better for me, I thought. I shouldn't have been saved from the fire, brought here to suffer, and now take such a long time to die to deliver me from my shame and my family's."[37] While Souad survived the attempted murder, she was forced to endure great suffering in her long battle back to health. Finally, she moved to Europe where she now lives with her husband and three children.[38] Remarkably, her telling of the story concludes with her being reunited with the child of her pregnancy, a son, with whom she was burned years before.

Similarly, both Saeeda Khanum and Danielle Lurie have directed films addressing honor killings. In 2004, Lurie directed the 10 minute short drama, *In the Morning*.[39] In 2005, Khanum directed *Love, Honor & Disobey* for Faction Films. Khanum's film addresses domestic violence in various forms, from physical abuse to forced marriages to honor killings. Similarly, In 1998, Shelley Saywell, Sonja Smits, and Arsinée Khanjian produced the film, *Crimes of Honour*. This 44-minute program documents the killing of sisters or daughters suspected of losing their virginity, for having refused an arranged marriage, and having left a husband. The movie also emphasizes that even if a woman is raped, abused, or is the victim of gossip, she may pay the terrible price.[40]

Finally, I opened the introduction to this book with a poem by an Iraqi feminist, Nazik al-Malaika. In the poem, we are confronted with the violent crime of honor killings in a powerful manner. For the poet, it is not enough to simply describe or define the act. We must hear the monster say, "We killed her." We must also wonder with the women, "And tomorrow, who knows which desert swallows us, to wash off shame?" It is through such a poem, through various narratives, and through documentary films that we gain a more detailed and rich perspective on the reality of honor killings.

37. Ibid., 101.
38. Her husband is not the man with whom she had the affair.
39. The 2004 film, *In the Morning*, is in Turkish with English sub-titles.
40. See also *Honor Killings* and *Our Honour, His Glory*.

Virginity, Patriarchy, and Hymenorraphy[41]

It is impossible to overstate the importance of a woman's virginity in the patriarchal societies of the Middle East and the Mediterranean world. Suzanne Ruggi explains that "a woman's virginity is the property of the men around her, first her father, later a gift for her husband; a virtual dowry as she graduates to marriage. In this context, a women's *'ard* (honor) is a commodity which must be guarded by a network of family and community members."[42] Furthermore, the guarding of this "commodity" is an essential component for male identity and family honor.

> . . . virginity is a matter between men, in which women merely play the role of silent intermediaries. Like honour, virginity is the manifestation of a purely male preoccupation in societies where inequality, scarcity, and the degrading subjection of some people to others deprive the community as a whole of the only true human strength: self-confidence. The concepts of honour and virginity locate the prestige of a man between the legs of a woman. It is not by subjugating nature or by conquering mountains and rivers that a man secures his status, but by controlling the movements of women related to him by blood or by marriage, and by forbidding them any contact with male strangers.[43]

Mernissi's use of vibrant and vivid language highlights a salient feature of the relationship between virginity and patriarchy. This is perhaps nowhere better seen than in Arabic vocabulary. Sana al-Khayyat explains, "The Arabic word *adhra* (virgin) is a feminine word always used to refer to women, never to men; there is no masculine equivalent. When some of the women told me that their husbands 'had no sexual experience before marriage,' they had no convenient masculine term to use."[44] Without a word to describe their own lack of sexual experience, we witness again the male preoccupation with women's virginity.

In the patriarchal societies of the Middle East and the Mediterranean, the relationship between virginity and honor has forced some girls to

---

41. For a recent discussion of medical intervention and honor killings (both virginity testing and hymen reconstruction), see Parrot and Cummings, *Forsaken Females*, 183.

42. Ruggi, *Honor Killings in Palestine*, 13.

43. Mernissi, "Virginity and Patriarchy," 183.

44. al-Khayyat, *Honour and Shame*, 34.

consult doctors before marriage to ensure that their hymen is still intact.[45] While some girls are found to posses a typical hymen, others have an "elastic" hymen, which generally will not bleed. Still others are found to have a broken hymen from either sexual or non-sexual activity. In any case, those with a broken hymen do have a medical option. Fatima Mernissi introduces the practice of artificially restoring "virginity."

> It is no secret that when some marriages are consummated, the virginity of the bride is artificial. Enough young women to delight the gynecologists with the relevant skills, resort to a minor operation on the eve of their wedding in order to erase the traces of pre-marital experience. Before embarking on the traditional ceremonies of virginal modesty and patriarchal innocence, the young woman has to get a sympathetic doctor to wreak a magical transformation, turning her within a few minutes into one of Mediterranean man's most treasured commodities: the virgin, with hymen intact sealing a vagina which no man has touched.[46]

Mernissi continues by explaining the operation to restore virginity: "It is a matter of sewing up the remains of the hymen which remain even after repeated intercourse, and even after curettages and pregnancies. This operation which consists of a simple row of stitches, of which the number depends upon the state of the hymen, is known as *hymenorraphie*[47] or stitching of the remains of the hymen. When sutured, the hymen heals, and the woman miraculously becomes a virgin again."[48]

Like Mernissi and countless others, Jan Goodwin emphasizes the relationship between virginity, patriarchy, and family honor:

> The majority of Muslim women still find their lives controlled by their closest male relative. They are the daughters whose future marriage partners continue to be determined by their fathers. They are the brides who must be virgins on their wedding nights in a culture where if they are not, honor killings are common and often carried out by the girl's own brother.[49]

---

45. Ibid., 35.

46. Mernissi, *Virginity and Patriarchy*, 183.

47. While the spelling of this medical procedure varies (cf. hymenorraphie with hymenorrhaphy), the meaning and practice is the same.

48. Mernissi, *Virginity and Patriarchy*, 184.

49. Goodwin, *Price of Honour*, 32.

Goodwin also describes the practice of hymenorrhaphy, or hymen restoration. She notes that the practice, which is "quite common" in Jordan, helps to insure proof of virginity on the post-wedding night verification.[50]

How do the gynecologists who participate in such surgeries understand their role in this patriarchal obsession with virginity? Through an interview with Dr. Efteem Azar, one of Jordan's leading obstetricians/gynecologists, Goodwin invites us to consider the thoughts of some in the medical community. Azar explains, "You always have to favor the girl, because if you don't, she'll be killed by her family. Sometimes, if the girl has the opportunity, she'll beg you to cover for her. They are very frightened, they know they will be killed. So you tell the male relatives the bride had an elastic hymen, which many women do anyway, and in such cases she wouldn't bleed."[51] In this short, but very telling explanation, Azar again emphasizes the relationship between virginity, family honor, and the killing of girls.

In conclusion, the importance of a woman's virginity in the patriarchal societies of the Middle East and the Mediterranean cannot be overstated. Family honor depends on the chastity of its female members. Lama Abu-Odeh explains that this is also true throughout the Arab world, noting that writings about the importance of women's virginity before marriage abound.[52] While many before have emphasized the importance of a woman's virginity, Abu-Odeh makes a striking connection between "bleeding in death" and "bleeding during sex":

> Arab women, according to the ideal model, are expected to abstain from any kind of sexual practice before they get married. The hymen, in this context, becomes the socio-physical sign that both assures, guarantees virginity and gives the woman a stamp of respectability and virtue. The wedding night, therefore, bears phenomenal importance for Arab women, since it is that crucial time when society is about to make a judgment on their property. Some honour crimes are known to occur precisely then, when a woman's failure to bleed as a result of penetration to break her hymen, is taken as a failure of the social test . . . [alternatively] she [might be] "taken back" by the groom and his family to her own family, who

50. Ibid., 279.

51. Ibid.

52. Abu-Odeh directs readers to the following texts regarding the issue of virginity and marriage in the Arab world: Saadawi, *The Hidden Face of Eve*; Abu-Lughod, *Veiled Sentiments*; Combs-Schilling, *Sacred Performances*; and Gilmore, *Honor and Shame*.

in turn might kill her for having shamed them. Only her bleeding
in death can erase the shame brought about by her failure to bleed
during sex on her wedding night.[53]

In graphic detail, Abu-Odeh again emphasizes both the necessity of a women's virginity and the consequences of pre-marital sexual activity.

Honor Killing

A Survey by the Palestinian Center for Public Opinion

How do modern Palestinians feel about honor killings? The answer to this question will prove essential to this chapter for two reasons. First, we will see that many Palestinians continue to support a family's right to kill a female member to preserve family honor. Second, we will also see that there are men and women who oppose honor killings and consider the practice to be a serious social problem. The two opposing viewpoints help us both to understand the reality of honor killings and to fight against the tendency for neocolonialism by acknowledging opposition to the practice.

In May 2002, The Palestinian Center for Public Opinion in Beit-Sahour carried out a survey on behalf of the Palestinian Human Rights Monitoring Group in Jerusalem.[54] The main objective of the survey was to discover the views of the Palestinian public regarding the phenomenon of killing women on the basis of family honor. When asked if they realized that a woman was involved in an honor related case (e.g., committing adultery), 25.9 % of males responded that "the family should kill her to wipe out the disgrace," while 16.3 percent of females support such an honor killing. Similarly, when asked whether or not the killing of a woman would wipe out a disgrace, 26.7% of the respondents answered positively.

Next, the respondents were asked whether or not a family has the right to kill a female on the basis of family honor, 25.3% of males and 15.4% of females "strongly agreed." Furthermore, 18.6% of males and 16.3% of females "somewhat agreed." Together, nearly 38% of the respondents felt that families have the right to participate in honor killings. Conversely, 58% percent of respondents opposed the right to kill females (3.6% answered that they "did not know"). In short, while the majority of respondents

53. Abu-Odeh, "Crimes of Honor," 149.
54. Palestinian Human Rights Monitoring Group, "Honor Killing."

oppose the killing of women in the name of family honor, well over one-third do support such an act.

Do honor killings deter other women from participating in acts which are detrimental to family honor? 28.2% of males and 20.1% of females "strongly agreed" that the killing of women suspected of harming the honor of the family may act as a deterrent. Furthermore, 23.1% of males and 19.9% of females "somewhat agreed." Together, just over 45% of the respondents felt that the killing of a woman would serve to deter other women from harming the honor of their families.

How long should the killer spend in prison for a crime of honor? 21.7% of males and 12.3% of females felt that the killer should not spend any time in prison. In addition, 10.3% of males and 10.5% of females felt that the killer should spend six months in prison. Finally, an additional 9.2% of males and 6.9% of females felt that the killer should spend one year in prison. Together, over 35% of respondents felt that the killer should spend between no time and one year in prison, while 30% felt that the killer should spend between one and ten years in prison (nearly 35% answered that they "did not know").

So what might we conclude from this study? As noted above, it is important to acknowledge the variety of views present in Palestine. The answers to each question indicate that there remains support for honor killings and for leniency in the punishment of such crimes. However, the answers also indicate an awareness of and opposition to this violent crime. The Palestinian Human Rights Monitoring Group draws several other important conclusions from the study. To begin, they understand that the practice of honor killings is due to "inherited culture."

> This study revealed that the inherited culture is still the major cri-
> teria that dominates the society, and controls the social views of
> the people in the society, especially in the subject of killing women
> on the basis of family honor. It was found that killing to save family
> honor is seen as a social disciplinary duty, and this was obvious in
> the wide support for women to wear the veil and gown, and the
> strong support for separation between men and women in many
> activities.[55]

While "inherited culture" is understood to be the cause for honor killings, The Palestinian Human Rights Monitoring Group also notes that education

---

55. Ibid.

and religion do not seem to be factors in one's view of the crime. They note, "We also discovered that educational level and the commitment to religion was not very influential on the issue of honor killing. The ideas of secular people, religious and traditional people were almost the same in most of the aspects of the subject."[56] In short, honor killings appear to be a practice inherited through culture and not informed or impacted by education or religious beliefs.

Honor Killings: Religious or Cultural Practice?

The conclusions of The Palestinian Human Rights Monitoring Group raise an essential question when considering the practice of honor killings, "Are honor killings a religious or a cultural practice?" Worded differently, and much more frankly, "Are honor killings a Muslim practice?" Perhaps another neocolonialist tendency among North Atlantic individuals is to view the practice of honor killings as a "Muslim issue." Simply stated, this view is incorrect. Honor killings are practiced by Hindus, Sikhs, Christians, Jews, and Muslims. In fact, in a 2006 poll, one in ten British Asians responded that honor killings are justifiable. According to the Agence France Press, "A tenth of 500 Hindus, Sikhs, Christians and Muslims surveyed by the BBC's Asian Network radio said they would condone the murder of someone who disrespected their family's honor."[57] Similarly, Newell, her colleagues, and the Youth Advocate Program International emphasize that the practice of honor killings is not limited to Muslims. They note, "Arab Christians, a minority in the Middle East, also commit honor killings. Experts say that Arab Christians commit honor killings in proportion to their population in the Middle East."[58] Newell and her associates are also quick to point out that while honor killings do occur in both Muslim and Christian communities, the practice is not dictated by the religious doctrine of either group.

Recent newspaper stories also show religious diversity in the practice of honor killings. In May 2007, David Ward, a reporter for *The Guardian* (London), told the story of an honor killing within a Sikh family: "A young woman was murdered by her husband and his mother because they thought

---

56. Ibid.

57. Agence France Press, "One in 10 British Asians backs honour killings: poll."

58. Newell et al., *Discrimination Against the Girl Child*, 22.

she had brought disgrace on their Sikh family by seeking a divorce."[59] In July 2005, Chris McGreal, also a reporter for *The Guardian*, told the story of an honor killing within a Christian family.

> Faten Habash's father wept as he assured her there would be no more beatings, no more threats to her life, and that she was free to marry the man she loved, even if he was a Muslim. All he asked was that Faten return home. Hassan Habesh even gave his word to an emissary from a Bedouin tribe traditionally brought in to mediate in matters of family honour, a commitment regarded as sacrosanct in Palestinian society. But the next weekend, as Faten watched a Boy Scouts parade from the balcony of her Ramallah home, the 22-year-old Christian Palestinian was dragged into the living room and bludgeoned to death with an iron bar. Her father was arrested for the murder.[60]

For both Ward and McGreal, the stories of honor killings dealt with the cultural values of family honor and its patriarchal control over women's sexuality regardless of religious beliefs.

In her discussion of the deep cultural roots of honor killings, Suzanne Ruggi emphasizes that the practice emerged in the ancient patriarchal and patrilineal societies of the Middle East. Ruggi develops her explanation by quoting Sharif Kanaana, professor of anthropology at Birzeit University.

> It is, [Kanaana] believes, "a complicated issue that cuts deep into the history of Arab societies." He argues that the honor killing stemmed from the patriarchal and patrilineal society's interest in maintaining strict control over designated familial power structures. "What the men of the family, clan, or tribe seek control of in a patrilineal society is reproductive power. Women for the tribe were considered a factory for making men. The honor killing is not a means to control sexual power or behavior. What's behind it is the issue of fertility, or reproductive power."[61]

In other words, it is not religious doctrine or beliefs that dictate the practice of honor killings, but the centuries old patriarchal concern for power over women and their reproductive rights.

---

59. Ward, "Sikh wife's affair sparked honour killing by husband and his mother," 4.
60. McGreal, "Murder in the name of family honour," 18.
61. Ruggi, *Honor Killings in Palestine*, 13.

Shahrzad Mojab offers a helpful critique when discussing the nature of honor killings. In response to a Kurdish honor killing case, Mojab warns against asking whether honor killings are "cultural" or "religious":

> This new case of honor killing has brought up old questions such as "Is honor killing part of Kurdish culture?" Or, "Is it a religious, Islamic, phenomenon?" There are many political and theoretical underpinnings to these questions. While I argue that violence against women should not be reduced to a question of culture, I also believe "honor killing" is definitely part and parcel of the culture of Kurdistan, and other societies in which it is practiced. However, reducing this crime to culture, may readily lead to racist interpretations and appropriations.[62]

Taking the warning of Mojab seriously, I intend for this book to work against the grain of neocolonialism and I do not suggest that "only other cultures" participate in violence against women. I do, however, want to emphasize that honor killings are not "religious" in nature, but are grounded in a patriarchal desire to control female sexuality and reproduction.

Honor Killings and the Discrepancy between Legality and Reality

It is beyond the scope of this book to discuss the many laws concerning honor killings. While I have noted above that some have emphasized the leniency shown to the men involved in honor killings, I will not outline either the laws or the sentencing relating to this violent crime. I do, however, wish to draw your attention to an important study which explores the context of women's sexuality in Eastern Turkey.[63] In this study, Pinar Ikkaracan and the Women for Women's Human Rights emphasize the discrepancy between legality and reality for women in Eastern Turkey.

Ikkaracan explains that Turkey is unique with respect to the extent of progressive reforms of the family code affecting women's lives.

> In 1926 the introduction of the Turkish Civil Code, based on the Swiss Civil Code, banned polygamy and granted women equal rights in matters of divorce, child custody and inheritance.

62. Mojab, "'Honor Killing': Culture, Politics, and Theory," 1–2.
63. Ikkaracan, "Exploring the Context of Women's Sexuality in Eastern Turkey," 66–75.

However, even several decades after these reforms, customary and religious practices continue to be more influential in the daily lives of the majority of women living in Turkey than the civil code; this is especially the case for women living in Eastern Turkey.[64]

In other words, although Turkey is progressive in its laws regarding women's rights, women themselves feel that their lives are governed by customs and religious practices that stand at odds with Turkish law.

Ikkaracan explains the gulf between the official laws in Turkey and the actual practice of honor killings:

> At the present time, there are no official laws in Turkey restricting the right of a women to engage in a relationship with any man or women of her choice before, during, or after marriage. However, extra-marital relationships are an absolute taboo for women in the region, whereas men's extra-marital affairs are widely accepted and even socially 'legalised' in many cases through the institution of polygyny. The customary penalty for women suspected of such a crime in the region is usually death, the so-called honour killings.[65]

Here, Ikkaracan explains that even though there are no laws in Turkey restricting women from engaging in an extra-marital relationship, the customary penalty for such activity is usually death. This discrepancy, the gulf between legality and reality, has encouraged women in Eastern Turkey to misunderstand, and even mistrust, their own progressive laws. Ikkaracan continues by emphasizing that the perception of women in Eastern Turkey is often very different from the legal reality.

> A majority of the women (66.6 per cent) believed that, contrary to the law, they could not divorce their husbands if [their husband] committed adultery, even if they would have liked to . . . although the increase in women's educational levels increased women's perception of the possibility of getting a divorce, 31.5 per cent of women who had secondary or higher education still believed they could not divorce their husbands for adultery. Interestingly, there was no difference in the perceptions of women living in urban and rural areas on the issue.[66]

64. Ibid., 66.
65. Ibid., 71.
66. Ibid., 72.

In other words, although the law allows for women to divorce their husbands, the perception for two thirds of the women in Eastern Turkey is that this is not possible.

So, what is the significance of this study? At one level, we are made aware that the practice of honor killing is not one that can be easily halted through legislation. However, on another level, we are made aware that there is often a great divide between practice and the law and between perception and the law. When biblical interpreters examine the birth narrative in the gospel of Matthew, there is often discussion regarding first-century divorce law. This study encourages us to push beyond this legal discussion and inquire about the actual lives, perceptions and practices of first-century Palestinians.

Conclusion

Honor killings are the murder of girls and women who are thought to have damaged the honor of their families. Through premarital or extramarital sexual activity, these girls or women are believed to have brought public disgrace to the family and the mark of their shame must be erased. In many cases, this involves the killing of the girl or woman. While this definition is correct, it is also insufficient. Girls and women are also killed in cases or rape and child sexual abuse. In a world where perception is often reality, even flirting or mere allegations of improper behavior on the part of a girl or woman are often enough to defile a family's honor and "warrant" an honor killing. Such crimes must be understood as human rights violations and understood in the global context and discussion of women's rights. Furthermore, we must not be tempted to understand honor killings in terms of ethnicity or religion. Hindus, Sikhs, Christians, Jews, and Muslims from many countries participate in this violent crime. While the killing of women is still practiced and supported by many, there is growing opposition to this practice.

2

"Joseph's Dilemma"

THE MANY AND DIVERSE interpretations of the birth narrative of Jesus in Matthew's gospel seem to include every detail and possible variant reading except that of an honor killing. Interpreters debate the virginal conception,[1] whether or not Joseph suspected Mary of adultery,[2] the nature of divorce in first-century Palestine,[3] and what it means that Joseph was "righteous."[4]

1. For an early example of this discussion, see Taylor, *The Historical Evidence for the Virgin Birth*. For a more recent text, see Lüdemann, *Virgin Birth?*.

2. This topic will be discussed in detail below. For an example of an interpreter who assumes that Joseph did not suspect Mary of adultery, see Hendrickx, *The Infancy Narratives*, 31–32. For an example of an interpreter who assumes that Joseph did suspect Mary of adultery, see Schaberg, *The Illegitimacy of Jesus*, 44–45; or Tosato, "Joseph, Being a Just Man (Matt 1:19)," 547–51. For a thorough overview of this discussion, see Calkins, "The Justice of Joseph Revisited," 165–77.

3. Many interpreters offer a description of marriage and divorce in first-century Palestine. For a description of the "legal situation Matthew depicts," see Schaberg, *The Illegitimacy of Jesus*, 42–62. For a recent and thorough description of divorce in the Bible, see Instone-Brewer, *Divorce and Remarriage in the Bible: The Social and Literary Context*.

4. The "righteousness" of Joseph is commonly interpreted in one of two ways. First, does Joseph's righteousness consist of his faithfulness to the law? Second, is Joseph righteous because he does not want to shame Mary? In other words, does his mercy reveal his righteousness? For a brief overview of this discussion, see Hagner, *Matthew 1–13*, 18; or Luz, *Matthew 1–7*, 95. Please note that the Luz text has been published by

The genealogy of Jesus in the first chapter of Matthew is mined for clues.[5] The social world of the New Testament is considered.[6] Does Joseph act honorably?[7] The Greek text is translated and re-translated.[8] Some interpreters hint that the penalty for adultery was severe, or that death was threatened.[9] And yet, with so much attention given to the birth story, with so much written about Mary, Joseph, and Jesus, the very real possibility of an honor killing has not been considered. As thousands of girls and women continue to die each year in honor killings, North Atlantic biblical interpreters seem to imagine a world where such violence does not and did not exist. In this chapter, I will outline many of the modern interpretations of the birth narrative in Matthew's gospel. Further, I will examine what others consider to be Joseph's dilemma. In the end, we will find that while there is diversity in the reading of the text, there is one important shared characteristic: there is silence regarding the very real practice of honor killings.

T. & T. Clark (Edinburgh) and in the Hermeneia commentary series (Minneapolis: Fortress). The page numbers used in this footnote and throughout this book refer to the T. & T. Clark edition (see bibliography).

5. For examples of this discussion, see Freed, "The Women in Matthew's Genealogy," 3–19; Nolland, "The Four (Five) Women and Other Annotations in Matthew's Genealogy," 527–39; or Weren, "The Five Women In Matthew's Genealogy," 288–305.

6. See Horsley, *The Liberation of Christmas*; Malina and Rorhbaugh, *Social-Science Commentary on the Synoptic Gospels*, 26–31; or Pilch, *The Cultural World of Jesus*, 10–12.

7. This question is addressed by Malina and Rorhbaugh in their discussion of the "righteousness" of Joseph. Malina and Rorhbaugh, *Social-Science Commentary on the Synoptic Gospels*, 26.

8. A comparison of translations is fascinating and often reveals a great deal about the assumptions of the translators. For example, the New Revised Standard Version translates Matt 1:19 as, "Her husband Joseph, being a righteous man and unwilling to expose her to public disgrace, planned to dismiss her quietly." In contrast, Ivor H. Jones offers a translation which makes explicit his assumption that the context of Joseph's dilemma was that of divorce. According to Jones, Matt 1:19 reads "Being a man of principle, and at the same time wanting to save her from exposure, Joseph made up his mind to have the marriage contract quietly set aside." Jones, *The Gospel of Matthew*, 4. Furthermore, it is interesting that Jones uses the word, "exposure." From the context of his translation, it is impossible to discern what he means by this term. Does he me exposure to public shame? Or, does he mean exposure to death?

9. For an example, see Argyle, *The Gospel According to Matthew*, 28.

Joseph Reacts to Mary's Pregnancy[10]

The discussion of Joseph's dilemma typically begins with his awareness of and reaction to Mary's pregnancy. Three proposals are commonly identified.[11] First, it is proposed that Joseph *suspected Mary of adultery*.[12] Second, some suggest that Joseph did not suspect Mary of adultery, nor did he know anything about her miraculous conception. Rather, Joseph *suspended all judgment*.[13] Finally, it is proposed that Joseph was aware of Mary's miraculous conception by the Holy Spirit. He, in turn, *was filled with awe and feared to take Mary as his wife*.[14] While interpreters commonly choose one of the three proposals regarding Joseph's awareness of and reaction to Mary's pregnancy, it is only the first proposal that lends itself to the possible discussion of honor killings.[15] If Joseph did suspect Mary of adultery, his dilemma involved choosing between the options of punishment for such an act. However, if Joseph suspended judgment or was aware that Mary's pregnancy was miraculous in nature, the discussion of an honor killing would seem absurd. Therefore, my thesis, that the context of the birth narrative in

10. For a summary of Joseph's reaction to Mary's pregnancy in the Gospel of Matthew, the *Protevangelium of James*, the *Gospel of Pseudo-Matthew*, the *Gospel of the Birth of Mary*, and the *History of Joseph the Carpenter*, see Elliot, *A Synopsis of the Apocryphal Nativity and Infancy Narratives*, 43–44.

11. While the majority of interpreters envision three primary proposals for Joseph's awareness of and reaction to Mary's pregnancy, other proposals are offered. For example, G. E. P. Cox concludes that it does not matter whether Mary had committed adultery or not, Joseph must divorce her. He explains, "We need not too lightly assume that Joseph was convinced of Mary's guilt, which is the usual interpretation of his bewilderment. But whether she was an adulteress or a chosen vessel of God, she was no longer to be his, and as a 'righteous man' (R.V.) he was resolved upon privately giving her a deed of cancellation." Cox, *The Gospel According to Saint Matthew*, 29.

12. For an example, see Davies, *Matthew*, 32. "Readers infer that Joseph regarded Mary's pregnancy as evidence of her union with another man, and his quiet release of her from the betrothal would have left her free to marry her child's father."

13. For a succinct summary of this position, see Calkins, "The Justice of Joseph Revisited," 169–71.

14. Hendrickx, *The Infancy Narratives*, 31–32. See also, Calkins, "The Justice of Joseph Revisited," 165–77.

15. The denominational affiliation of the interpreter often dictates which proposal is supported. For example, while most Protestants assume the first proposal (that Joseph suspected Mary of adultery), Roman Catholics tend to support the second or, more commonly, the third. Roman Catholic, Raymond Brown, is a notable exception (see Brown, *The Birth of the Messiah*, 122–28).

Matthew is that of a possible honor killing, depends upon Joseph suspecting Mary of adultery.

In 1936, F. W. Green boldly declared that, "all modern commentators are agreed, the words [of Matthew 1:19] clearly mean that Joseph believed from the beginning in Mary's innocence."[16] In 1975, Herman Hendrickx echoed Green. He noted that, "most modern commentators do not accept the view that Joseph suspected Mary."[17] While the confidence of Green and Hendrickx is unquestionable, their conclusion is not. In fact, that Joseph suspected Mary of adultery is clearly the majority opinion for modern interpreters. Jane Schaberg offers a powerful description and defense of this position.[18]

> The logic and structure of the story are violated if we assume with some critics that before the encounter with the angel Joseph knew that the pregnancy was "through the Holy Spirit." This theory requires the reader to guess blindly at the source of Joseph's information, and to presume that "religious awe" would lead him to decide on divorce. It also makes redundant, anticlimactic, and nonrevelatory the angel's words to him at the end of v 20: "what is begotten in her is through the Holy Spirit." It is better to understand the first mention of the Spirit in v 18 as an explanation Matthew addresses to the reader, which is "not part of the narrative flow." Matthew wants the reader at this point to know more than Joseph does.[19]

Here, Schaberg convincingly argues that the text of Matthew reveals Joseph's assumption of the adultery of Mary.

It is not, however, only modern interpreters who hold this view. Arthur Burton Calkins explains that, "We also find the hypothesis of adultery held most probably even prior to the *Protoevangelium of James*[20] by St. Justin Martyr (ca. 165) in his *Dialogue with Trypho*. This position was also given most powerful backing in the preaching of two of the great Western Fathers of the Church, St. Ambrose (339–397) and St. Augustine (354–430) and by

---

16. F. W. Green, *The Gospel According to St Matthew*, 104.

17. Hendrickx, *The Infancy Narratives*, 31.

18. It seems that Schaberg is deeply indebted to the interpretation of Raymond Brown. See Brown, *The Birth of the Messiah*, 122–28.

19. Schaberg, *The Illegitimacy of Jesus*, 44–45.

20. This important text, more commonly titled the *Protevangelium of James*, will receive significant attention in chapter 3.

probably the greatest father of the East, St. John Chrysostom (354–407)."[21] Calkins further notes that an ancient Greek hymn also supports this position. He explains, "The Akathistos Hymn of the Greek Church dating from the late fifth or early sixth century in its third kontakion also accepts the hypothesis that Joseph suspected adultery."[22]

Why have so many early readers of Matthew, together with most modern readers, concluded that Joseph suspected Mary of adultery? Quite simply, the narrative flow of the text requires the reader to come to this conclusion. In v. 18, readers are provided with information that is not known to Joseph. Mary is with child—through the Holy Spirit. Raymond Brown explains, "Matthew wants the reader to know more than do the characters in the story, so that the reader will not entertain for a moment the suspicion that grows in Joseph's mind."[23] While we, as readers, do not face a dilemma, it is clear from the text that Joseph does. The dilemma continues until an angel of the Lord appears to Joseph in a dream (vv. 20–21). Since the text itself makes real the dilemma faced by Joseph, we too must closely consider this dilemma.

Returning to the conclusions of Jane Schaberg, she correctly identifies that, "Adultery or rape are two normal alternatives Joseph had for explaining the pregnancy with which he was confronted."[24] Further, Schaberg adds that, "two alternative actions were considered by him: to expose Mary to public shame or to divorce her secretly—the action he chose."[25] In the end, while Schaberg does correctly identify the context of Joseph's dilemma, the possibility of an honor killing is never considered.

---

21. Calkins, "The Justice of Joseph Revisited," 166–67. It is important to note that although Calkins offers a thorough and helpful description of the history of the "hypothesis of adultery," he concludes, with many other Roman Catholic interpreters, that Joseph experienced "reverential fear." Calkins, "The Justice of Joseph Revisited," 171–77.

22. Ibid., 167.

23. Brown, *The Birth of the Messiah*, 124.

24. Schaberg, *The Illegitimacy of Jesus*, 45. Schaberg is not alone in her argument that Joseph might have suspected that Mary was raped. For another example, see Buchanan, *The Gospel of Matthew*, 73. Buchanan notes, "Joseph might have considered Mary to be a suspected adulteress and have taken her to the priest and had her tested for faithfulness (Numbers 5), but he did not. The mythologist presented Joseph as one who probably thought Mary had been innocently raped and chose not to embarrass her further, but instead to divorce her quietly."

25. Ibid., 45.

What Were Joseph's Options?

The central question facing readers of Matt 1:19 is simple, "If Joseph suspected Mary of adultery, what were his options?" The text indicates that Joseph is confronted with the pregnancy of Mary (and makes clear his subsequent assumption of adultery, for they have not yet begun to live together and he has not yet been told that Mary is with child through the Holy Spirit). This is, of course, the context of Joseph's dilemma. The dilemma itself is the choice between different and rival options. In other words, what options does a "righteous" man have when he is confronted with the adultery of his wife? While all interpreters seem to agree that divorce was an option, there is surprisingly little discussion or consideration of other, rival options.[26] The question that dominates the discussion of Matt 1:19 is whether or not Joseph ought to make his divorce of Mary public or private? The stoning of Mary is commonly viewed as either anachronistic or is dismissed as shameful. The consideration that a formal court appearance was an option is also often dismissed in favor of the option of a private divorce. And the possibility of an honor killing has not been considered. In short, it is the threatened honor of *Mary* that seems to inform the interpretation of Matt 1:19.

That divorce was an option for Joseph is beyond dispute. In fact, not only do most (if not all) interpreters assume that divorce was an option, many write as if it was the only option. The dilemma, then, is the choice between a "public" or "private" divorce. A public divorce, it is believed would bring shame upon Mary. A private divorce would minimize her disgrace. Floyd V. Filson offers an example of such a reading:

> Since betrothal was legally binding, Joseph is called **her husband** (vs. 19) and Mary **your wife** and **his wife** (vss. 20, 24). To break the bond Joseph would have to divorce her. He thought that Mary had violated the marriage tie by sinful relations with another man. In his uprightness he thought divorce necessary, but with a kindly concern to cause Mary a minimum of shame and public disgrace he **decided to divorce her secretly**, with the minimum number of legal witnesses (two, in rabbinical sources).[27]

26. There are interpretations that do not seem to envision rival options or do not explicitly mention divorce. For example, Charles Erdman offers a short commentary on the birth of Jesus. With regard to Matt 1:19, he simply notes that, "the mother of Jesus is about to be repudiated . . ." Erdman, *The Gospel of Matthew*, 25.

27. Filson, *A Commentary on the Gospel According to St. Matthew*, 54. See also Fenton, *Saint Matthew*, 43; Garland, *Reading Matthew*, 21; Hare, *Matthew*, 9; Keener, *A*

For Filson, that Joseph will divorce Mary is without question. And, without any other options provided, the dilemma involves only the public/private nature of the divorce. It is important to note that he does not envision the killing of Mary as an option. Furthermore, when he does mention "shame," Joseph's actions are motivated by minimizing the shame of Mary and not, as we would expect, the defense of *his* honor.

R. T. France echoes Filson's conclusion that Joseph would divorce Mary. However, France does include another option that he writes off as anachronistic. France notes that while Deuteronomy prescribes the punishment of stoning for those that have committed adultery, he asserts that this practice was no longer in use at the turn of the first-century.

> In Old Testament law the penalty for unchastity before marriage was stoning (Dt. 22:13–21), but by this time divorce, based on Deuteronomy 24:1, was the rule . . . Joseph, as *a just (i.e.* law-abiding) *man*, could, and perhaps should, have done so by accusation of adultery resulting in a public trail, but his unwillingness to *put her to shame* . . . led him to consider the permitted alternative of private divorce before two witnesses.[28]

France was not the first, nor the last to claim that stoning was no longer practiced in the first century. Francis Wright Beare boldly declares that, "There is no evidence that this penalty was imposed at the time of the Gospel, but a public repudiation would certainly bring lasting shame upon the woman."[29] Ironically, neither France nor Beare provide any evidence that stoning did *not* occur in the first century. Not only is there a complete lack of evidence to support their claim, but neither interpreter attempts to explain the related story of Jesus and the woman caught in adultery (John 8:1–11). Finally, it is again the interplay between the honor of Mary and the public/private nature of divorce which is perceived to be Joseph's dilemma.

Similarly, Ulrich Luz notes that, "According to Deut 22:23f., stoning was obligatory punishment for the adultery of betrothed persons. However, it was no longer practiced at that time."[30] What makes Luz's comment so important is that he *does* attempt to offer evidence. Luz refers to a 1922

Commentary on the Gospel of Matthew, 90–91; and Witherington, *Women in the Early Church*, 166–69.

28. France, *The Gospel According to Matthew*, 77.

29. Beare, *The Gospel according to Matthew*, 68.

30. Luz, *Matthew 1–7*, 119.

text by Hermann Leberecht Strack and Paul Billerbeck.[31] Unfortunately, Strack and Billerbeck do not claim that stoning was no longer practiced in the first century. In fact, the opposite claim is made. In their commentary on Matt 1:19 in light of the Mishnah and Talmud, Strack and Billerbeck explain that it was not permitted to kill a *minor* if she committed adultery. However, they further note, that a girl who has committed adultery and is at least 12 years, 6 months, and 1 day old, may be killed by either stoning or strangulation. In other words, the evidence that Luz does provide in no way claims that stoning was no longer practiced in the first century.[32] Robert H. Gundry repeats the claim made by Luz, noting that, "Because he wanted to keep the Mosiac law, Joseph considered himself obligated at least to divorce Mary (Deut 22:23–24). Some rabbinic evidence suggests relaxation of the prescribed stoning . . ."[33] Again following the lead of Luz, Gundry refers to the work of Strack and Billerbeck. The point cannot be made strongly enough, Strack and Billerbeck do not state in any way that stoning was no longer practiced in the first century. What is most troublesome about the interpretations of Luz and Gundry is not their misrepresentation of Strack and Billerbeck, it is their apparent lack of awareness of the very real ancient and continuing threat to women and girls who are thought to have shamed their families.

Another scenario for Joseph's dilemma involves the choice between divorcing Mary and bringing her before a court of law to be tried and sentenced. Arthur Carr offers an early example of this position. He writes, "But two courses were open to him. He could either summon her before the law-courts to be judicially condemned and punished, or he could put her away by a bill of divorcement before witnesses, but without assigning cause."[34] While Carr mentions "punishment," he offers no description of what this might be. We might presume that he is referring to the proscribed stoning of Deut 22:23–24, but this is never made explicit. Furthermore, the assumption that Joseph will divorce Mary is again emphasized. Finally, Carr's conclusion that Joseph does not need to "assign cause" seems to reinforce the idea that the honor of Mary is at stake.

31. Luz cites pages 50–53 in the first volume of a six volume set entitled, *Kommentar zum Neuen Testament aus Talmud und Midrasch* (Str-B 1.50–53).

32. Strack and Billerbeck, *Kommentar zum Neuen Testament aus Talmud und Midrasch*, 1.50–53.

33. Gundry, *Matthew*, 21.

34. Carr, *The Gospel According to St Matthew*, 83.

Some interpreters do not dismiss the punishment of death as anachronistic. However, divorce is described as being the less "shameful" of the forms of punishment. In 1996, Warren Carter noted, "Deuteronomic law allowed death for intercourse with a betrothed woman (Deut 22:23–27). Joseph, not aware of the Spirit's role and assuming Mary to be pregnant by another man, decides not to put her to death but to exercise a less shameful action of divorcing her quietly."[35] Again, it is the honor of Mary that seems to be threatened and not the honor of her family. Furthermore, it is the act of killing that is described as being "shameful," not the adultery itself. Ironically, Warren Carter interpreted Matt 1:19 four years later and made no mention of the possibility of the death of Mary. He explained that, "In Joseph's view, Mary has dishonored him by violating the betrothal agreement. Divorce is the only option (cf. Deut 22:20–27). But righteousness or justice is not separated from mercy, so *not wishing to expose her to public disgrace*, Joseph prefers a quiet divorce."[36] In his 2000 reading of Matt 1:19, Carter boldly proclaims that divorce is the "only option." In doing so, he returns to the public/private divorce option explored earlier by Filson. Carter also associates a public divorce with the undesirable shaming of Mary.

Similarly, Daniel J. Harrington takes seriously the option of stoning. "The . . . term [righteous] is best interpreted with reference to Joseph's observance of the Law . . . The particular law that concerned Mary and Joseph appears in Deut 22:23–27, the case of an engaged woman found not to be a virgin. She was to be returned to her father's house and stoned to death by the men of the city on account of the disgrace brought upon her father's house."[37] Harrington continues, however, by returning to the now common theme of the honor of Mary. He notes that, "Joseph decided to spare Mary this public disgrace by simply putting her through the less public procedure of divorce . . ."[38] For Harrington, and countless others, the choices available to Joseph are evaluated in terms of their threat to the honor of Mary.

In light of the modern practice of honor killings, Joseph's options as envisioned by biblical interpreters seem quite problematic. On one hand, many interpreters seem to envision a world that is free from the violent killing of women. On the other hand, those that do entertain the possible

35. Carter, *Matthew: Storyteller, Interpreter, Evangelist*, 124.

36. Carter, *Matthew and the Margins*, 68.

37. Harrington, *The Gospel of Matthew*, 34.

38. Ibid., 34–35.

killing of Mary seem to misunderstand the dynamics of family honor and adultery in the ancient and modern Mediterranean world. Time and time again it is stated that a quiet divorce is the less shameful action and that Joseph would have been motivated to preserve the honor of Mary. Such readings are in direct opposition to the known practice of honor killings. Alessandra Antonelli, writing in the *Palestine Report*, reminds us, "Adultery has different meanings and consequences for men and women. The man has the 'right' to kill his wife and 'cleanse' his honor."[39] Antonelli continues by quoting Suad Abu Daya of the [Palestinian] Women's Center for Legal Aid and Counseling. Abu Daya explains that, "All the burden, even in cases of rape, is on the woman. She is the one who bears the consequences in any case, even by paying with her own life."[40]

It may seem shocking or scandalous to envision an honor killing as one of Joseph's options. However, in the following chapters I will argue that this is indeed the context that was assumed by early Christ-followers. Furthermore, the very real threat of an honor killing sets the narrative stage for Matthew's recurring theme that *from expected death comes unexpected new life*. Readers may wish to interpret Matt 1:19 in light of the threatened honor of Mary, but this does not reflect the reality of the punishment for adultery in the ancient world of Palestine or acknowledge the radical theme of "new life" in Matthew's gospel.

Studies on the Infancy Narratives[41]

For thirty years, Raymond E. Brown's classic text, *The Birth of the Messiah*, has served as the bedrock upon which modern biblical interpreters have built their understanding of the birth of Jesus. While interpreters have long been interested in the infancy narratives in Matthew and Luke, it is Brown's text that has become essential reading. Furthermore, Brown has both built upon and inspired many articles, chapters, and books which seek to explain the context and meaning of the birth of Jesus. In this section, I will

39. Antonelli, "Crimes not Stories," 16.

40. Ibid.

41. A wide variety of focused studies have been written concerning the infancy narratives in Matthew and Luke. Surprisingly, many do not address Joseph's dilemma. For an example, see Stendahl, *"Quis et Unde?"* 56–66.

explore Brown's commentary and four other contributions to the discussion of the birth narratives. As in the previous section, a single question will guide our inquiry. "What were Joseph's options?" More specifically, do these focused studies of the infancy narratives consider the possibility of an honor killing?

As noted above, Brown argues that Joseph suspected Mary of adultery. Readers of Matthew are told that Mary is pregnant through the Holy Spirit, but this information is only later revealed to Joseph.[42] In the meantime, he must decide what to do. According to Brown, Joseph is unwilling to "expose her to public disgrace." Unfortunately, Brown does not explain this public act. He does note that this is a "public display," but he fails to give any specific explanation of the shaming act.[43] Brown does, however, explain that Joseph intends to divorce Mary quietly. While a totally secret divorce is not possible ("since the writ of repudiation had to be delivered before two witnesses"),[44] Brown does understand the narrative to imply that Joseph will divorce Mary "leniently."[45] In other words, Joseph will not accuse Mary publicly of adultery and thus not subject her to a trial.[46]

So what options does Brown envision for Joseph? He clearly explains that Joseph suspects Mary of adultery. But, his explanation of Joseph's options is much less clear. For example, readers are never told what it means that Joseph is unwilling to expose Mary to public disgrace. In the end, Brown follows in the familiar footsteps of countless other interpreters. He describes a "quiet divorce," but does not give any substantive explanation of other options. Furthermore, Brown does not include a discussion of the possible stoning of Mary, nor does he include the possibility of an honor killing.[47]

Jean Daniélou offered an alternate reading of the birth stories in his text, *The Infancy Narratives.* Here, he addressed the topic of the virgin conception, Jesus' descent from David, and the prophecy of the Emmanuel.

42. Brown, *The Birth of the Messiah*, 124.

43. Ibid., 128.

44. Ibid.

45. Ibid.

46. Brown does add the following condition in reference to a trial: "If Num 5;11–31 was still effective in NT times, a trial by ordeal was the procedure when there was no witnesses to the adultery" (Ibid., 128).

47. For a helpful critique of Brown, see Bourke, review of *The Birth of the Messiah*, 120–24. Here, Bourke notes that, "The very existence in the first century of the Christian era of a 'less severe legal system' in which divorce rather than death was the required punishment is purely speculative . . ." Bourke, review of *The Birth of the Messiah*, 121.

Important for this study, Daniélou argues that Joseph did not suspect Mary of adultery. With this reading, there is no dilemma regarding what Joseph ought to do with his (presumed) adulterous wife. Rather, Joseph chooses to divorce Mary so that she is free to walk this "mysterious path" along which God was leading her.

> The story first shows [Joseph's] relationship with Mary, a relationship which has several successive stages. First, we have the betrothal of Joseph and Mary, and here Matthew confirms what we are told by Luke. Then, Joseph's attitude to Mary when he hears from her what God has revealed to her and what has taken place. Mary has become the instrument of God's mysterious plan, and thereby her feet are set on a very different path from anything he had expected. There is no question of his condemning her publicly, which he would have done if he were carrying out the Law which permitted the breaking-off of an engagement if the woman were unfaithful. Even if it were not for that reason, any official breaking-off would have cast an undeserved shadow of guilt on Mary. The only solution, then, was to leave her totally free to enter upon the mysterious path along which God was leading her.[48]

In this reading of the infancy narratives, Joseph does not suspect Mary of adultery and, therefore, the punishment of death is never mentioned. Similarly, Herman Hendrickx in his book, *Infancy Narratives*, does not address Joseph's dilemma. Like Daniélou, Hendrickx, argues that Joseph did not suspect Mary of adultery. It is not surprising, then, that Hendrickx does not discuss the possible options for punishment.[49]

R. T. France, in his text, "Scripture, Tradition, and History in the Infancy Narratives of Matthew," raises an important question, "But are these events credible in the real world of the first-century Palestine? Do they ring true?"[50] In other words, France encourages readers to consider the social context of the birth narratives. He wishes for readers to consider whether or not the stories reflect the real lives of first-century Mediterranean men and women. After considering both Joseph's dream and response and the flight to Egypt, France concludes that, "Joseph and his experiences ring true in the south-east Mediterranean world of the turn of the era, and the

48. Daniélou, *The Infancy Narratives*, 43

49. Hendrickx, *The Infancy Narratives*, 28–36.

50. France, "Scripture, Tradition, and History in the Infancy Narratives of Matthew," 255.

distinctive focus of these stories accords well with an origin in Joseph's own reminiscences."[51] Surprisingly, for a biblical interpreter interested in the social context of the birth stories, France never addresses Joseph's dilemma. Furthermore, he does not discuss either divorce or honor killings. So, while France urges his readers to consider the "real-world" context of the birth narratives, he himself is quite limited in his reading of the text.

Finally, René Laurentin, in his book, *The Truth of Christmas*, notes that Joseph was aware that Mary was pregnant and that the child belonged to God alone. Therefore, Joseph does not have a dilemma, for he knows that what has happened was the work of God. Joseph, in turn, "withdrew" so that Mary would not be placed in an awkward situation.

> This account by Matthew contains no hint of any suspicion on Joseph's part. His decision is explained by the fact that "he was a just man." If he had considered his wife to be guilty, justice would have demanded that he apply the Law to her; the Law, however, acknowledged no private proceedings but only an official writ of divorce (Dt 24:1). What Joseph knew, according to Matthew 1:18, is that this child belonged to God alone. Justice required that he not seek to make his own either the holy offspring that was not his or this wife who belonged to God. He therefore withdrew quietly to avoid putting Mary in an awkward situation. He left the resolution to God, the author of the event. The account gives no further details, as they are of no importance to the meaning.[52]

In short, Laurentin does not have to explain Joseph's dilemma, for Joseph does not suspect Mary of adultery. Since her pregnancy is always known to be the work of God, Joseph is not faced with a decision regarding adultery.

While the previous section explored Joseph's possible options as envisioned by a variety of biblical interpreters, each interpreter based their reading upon the assumption that Joseph suspected Mary of adultery. In sharp contrast, three of the five works outlined in this section are built around the assumption that Joseph did not suspect Mary of adultery. Because of this assumption, the possible punishment for adultery is not considered. While Raymond Brown does assume that Joseph suspects Mary of adultery, his discussion of her punishment is limited. Brown concludes rather vaguely that Joseph will divorce Mary leniently. Surprisingly, R. T. France does not

51. Ibid., 275.
52. Laurentin, *The Truth of Christmas*, 266.

even address Joseph's dilemma. In short, the readings of the infancy narratives outlined in this section either do not envision a dilemma for Joseph or do not offer a detailed description of Joseph's options. It is not surprising, then, that none consider the possibility of an honor killing.

Joseph's Dilemma and Social Scientific Interpretation

Biblical interpreters interested in the social world of the New Testament have raised the question of honor and the pregnancy of Mary.[53] Unfortunately, the relationship between honor and adultery continues to raise important questions. For social-scientific critics, it is again the honor of *Mary* that remains the focus. In other words, does Joseph offer a private divorce to defend *her* honor? As we have seen in the first chapter, it is *family* honor that is at risk. It seems, then, that the most appropriate option available to Joseph is that which defends the honor of the family, not the honor of Mary.

Bruce J. Malina and Richard L. Rohrbaugh in their text, *Social-Science Commentary on the Synoptic Gospels*, explain that, "virginity was the *sine qua non* for an honorable marriage. A woman without it would have shamed her entire paternal family."[54] While Malina and Rohrbaugh do identify the importance of virginity and family honor, they go on to define the dilemma of Joseph in terms of divorce and explain that a quiet divorce was offered so that he would not bring shame upon Mary.

> [Matt 1:19] . . . explains two things: why Joseph "planned to dismiss her" and to dismiss (divorce) her "quietly." The reason behind the first feature is that Joseph was a "righteous man," that is, a person who knew how to behave honorably in interpersonal relationships. Since the child Mary was carrying was not his, he would not usurp the right of another by taking it. By divorcing Mary, Joseph offered the real father of Jesus the opportunity of retrieving his child by marrying the mother. Moreover, he would carry out this divorce "quietly" because he was not willing to shame Mary. Clearly such

53. It is striking, however, that many social-scientific critics do not raise the issue of honor and the pregnancy of Mary. For example, Richard A. Horsely, in his text which examines the birth narratives, *The Liberation of Christmas*, does not deal with Joseph's dilemma. See Horsely, *The Liberation of Christmas*. Again, Jerome Neyrey in his text exploring honor and shame in the Gospel of Matthew does not deal with the issue of honor and shame and the pregnancy of Mary. See Neyrey, *Honor and Shame in Matthew*.

54. Malina and Rohrbaugh, *Social-Science Commentary on the Synoptic Gospels*, 26.

a motive indicates a decent and honorable person. To shame a female is to bring dishonor on her (and her family) by making a public verifiable accusation of unworthy behavior. For postmenarchic and premenopausal females, unworthy behavior is largely if not exclusively related to gender-based roles and sexual functions.[55]

In short, Malina and Rohrbaugh helpfully integrate the discussion of honor and shame into their interpretation of Matt 1:19. However, an important question remains: Why don't they consider whether or not the possibility of an honor killing acts as the broad cultural context for the interpretation of this verse?

That Malina and Rohrbaugh do not interpret Matt 1:19 in light of an honor killing is even more surprising when compared with Malina's discussion of honor and shame in his text, *Windows on the World of Jesus: Time Travel in Ancient Judea*.[56] Here, he explains that it is the oldest son's duty to restore the honor of the father in cases where a daughter dishonors her father and family.[57] In some cases, this involves the killing of the offending member of the family. Malina explains that the daughter "is considered as always bound, tied, connected with the father and the family. Her main concern is to act in a way that mirrors the values, concerns, and honor of her father and family."[58] When her actions are not mirror images of the family's values, she is dismissing his authority and the community will quickly deny the father's claim to social standing. In this case, the oldest son is responsible for restoring the family honor. Malina follows this discussion with many examples of the Bible's concern for "redemption," yet he never mentions the pregnancy of Mary. In short, Malina and Rohrbaugh helpfully describe the relationship between the virginity of women and family honor. Furthermore, they explain that when girls or women are believed to have shamed the family through inappropriate sexual behavior, it was the role of the oldest son to restore the family honor. Why, then, do they stop short of integrating this model of behavior into their reading of Matthew 1:19?

Similarly, John Pilch interprets Matt 1:19 in terms of Mary's honor. While he does mention the possible death of Mary, it is still the defense of

55. Ibid.

56. Malina, *Windows on the World of Jesus*, 1–19.

57. Malina provides helpful descriptions of Mediterranean cultural values by offering short fictional accounts followed by a detailed explanation. In this case, Malina uses the example of a woman eloping with her boyfriend. See ibid., 5–7.

58. Ibid., 5.

her honor that is the reason for a quiet divorce. Pilch, in his interpretation of "Joseph's predicament," notes three ways in which the values of honor and shame inform Matt 1:19. To begin, Pilch offers an interpretation very similar to that of Malina and Rohrbaugh. He notes that, "the honor code of the Mediterranean world demands that no one take what properly belongs to another. Mary's child is not Joseph's, so he hesitates to take it."[59] Next, Pilch notes that Joseph ". . . also knows that he will be unable to display publicly the 'tokens of virginity' (Deut 22:13–21) on his wedding night. If he doesn't act quickly, he will be shamed."[60] Finally, Pilch does note the possibility that Mary would be killed.

> By law, Joseph is entitled to return Mary to her father and expose her to death. Numbers 5:11–31 describes the ordeal Mary would have to undergo. But Joseph is an honorable man and determines to divorce her leniently. His sense of honor hopes that the rightful father will seize this opportunity to claim the child and marry Mary. In all his decision, Joseph acts very honorably.[61]

Pilch, like Malina and Rohrbaugh before him, describes the relationship between honor and adultery in the ancient Palestinian world. However, again like Malina and Rorhbaugh, he does not seem to consider that an honor killing (and the defense of *family* honor) is the most appropriate context in which to read the birth narrative in Matthew.

This book is deeply indebted to the work of Malina, Rorhbaugh, and Pilch. Without their foundational descriptions of honor and shame, I quite likely would not have considered an honor killing as the appropriate context for reading Matt 1:19. However, it is important to ask whether or not their interpretation of the relationship between honor and shame with the birth narrative in Matthew is the only (or even most appropriate) reading. Suzanne Ruggi, a staff reporter for *The Jerusalem Times*, repeatedly stresses the corporate nature of family honor and its dependence on the virginity of its unmarried female members. Stated simply, "a woman's virginity is the property of the men around her . . ."[62] When this virginity is lost, the honor of the family (and importantly, of the men) is in jeopardy. The result

---

59. Pilch, *The Cultural World of Jesus*, 11.

60. Ibid.

61. Ibid.

62. Ruggi, "Honor Killing in Palestine," 13.

is simple. It is the honor of the father and the family that must be defended, not that of the offending daughter.

Conclusion

The discussion of Joseph's dilemma begins with the question of his awareness of and reaction to Mary's pregnancy. The majority of modern biblical interpreters assume that Joseph suspected Mary of adultery. Furthermore, the interpreters focus their attention on the divorce of Mary. Will this divorce be public or private? It is the conclusion of most that the context of the birth narrative in Matthew's gospel is that of a private, quite, lenient divorce. Importantly, protecting the honor of Mary is the most common reason given for such a divorce. In other words, it is the honor of Mary that plays a central role in the interpretation of Matthew's birth narrative. Unfortunately, such a reading seems quite unlikely when considering the reality of honor killings. In the situation of adultery, it is the honor of the threatened family that is in jeopardy, not that of the offending girl. In cases both ancient and modern, it is the family honor that must be defended, even to the point of death.

3

Honor Killings in the Ancient Mediterranean World

IN THE FIRST CHAPTER, I described the practice of honor killings in the modern world. However, skepticism may remain that such violence occurred in the first century. Modern readers of the Bible are able to conceive of the violence of infanticide, persecution, and even crucifixion in the first century, but may not be willing to concede that brothers and fathers killed their sisters/daughters when family honor was at stake. In the New Testament, the Gospel of John tells a story of a woman caught in adultery who is about to be stoned,[1] and yet modern readers may be reluctant to believe that at that time a woman's sexual activity could lead to her death.

This chapter opens with a brief discussion by modern Palestinians and experts in the ancient Middle East who explain that the practice of honor killing is centuries old. Just as the modern patriarchal culture of Palestine emphasizes the relationship between virginity and family honor, the patriarchal culture of the ancient Mediterranean world also placed life-and-death importance on a girl's virginity. After this explanation of the roots of honor killings, I will offer many examples from ancient sources of the relationship between virginity and family honor. As we will see, this was not

1. John 8:1–11.

a theoretical discussion regarding the importance of virginity and chastity, but was a practical matter that carried deadly results. Finally, I will conclude this chapter with three early Christian interpretations of the birth story in Matthew. Here, it will be clear that it was assumed that Joseph's dilemma included the possible killing of Mary.

Before I begin, however, I must offer three important observations regarding the discussion of honor killings in the ancient Mediterranean world. First, the phrase "honor killing" is a modern English term. Therefore, ancient Greek and Latin texts will not use this specific designation for the killing of women and girls to defend family honor. That does not mean in any way that honor killings did not exist in the ancient Mediterranean world. It does mean, however, that we will not find the term in ancient Greek and Latin sources. Second, the practice of honor killings was, and continues to be, a family matter. It was not, and is not, part of a formal judicial process. In other words, a woman or girl who is thought to have threatened family honor did not, and does not, experience the formal process of a trial, sentencing, and punishment. Rather, families moved and continue to move quietly and quickly. Finally, and perhaps most importantly, it is essential to understand that honor killings were, and continue to be, public in one sense and private in another. The killing must be made public to the community. In other words, the community must know that the family defended its honor through the killing of the offending female member. However, once the community has been made aware of the action, the subject matter is then dropped. This makes researching ancient honor killings difficult, for the matter was made public to the community but was rarely documented. However, as this chapter will make clear, this silent and violent practice was most certainly a reality in the ancient Mediterranean world.

A Modern Discussion of the Ancient Practice of Honor Killings

A number of modern biblical interpreters have identified the importance of female virginity and chastity in the first-century Mediterranean world.[2]

---

2. Bruce J. Malina and Richard L. Rohrbaugh provide a helpful explanation of the punishment for adultery in the first century. See Malina and Rohrbaugh, *Social-Science Commentary on the Gospel of John*, 292–93. It is strange, however, that they describe the killing of adulterous women in their explanation of John 7:53—8:11, but do not consider

For example, Carolyn Osiek and Margaret Y. MacDonald explain that early Christianity created its own adaptation of the honor/shame code. Here, Osiek and MacDonald identify a standard for honorable conduct. Among the values identified as highly praised in early Christianity is that of female chastity.[3] While Osiek and MacDonald identify the importance of female chastity in the first century, they do not include a discussion of honor killings in their analysis. Similarly, Karen Jo Torjesen explains female honor in the first century Mediterranean world.

> The value placed on female shame is a common feature of patriarchal societies. When men give women in marriage, or when younger men acquire wives through some form of payment, women's sexuality is treated as a commodity. As a valuable economic good it must be controlled. Society therefore prescribes virginity for women before marriage and sexual fidelity after marriage, although it leaves male sexuality unregulated in both cases. The social control of women's sexuality produces a "feminine" personality conditioned by dependency. Furthermore, for patrilineal inheritance to work, a man had to know that the children his wife bore were his progeny, and only her chastity could guarantee this. Thus male anxiety about paternity led to the identification of shame and chastity as female virtues.[4]

Torjesen further indicates, "The chastity of female family members also affects the social world of a kinship group. Thus an entire family is disgraced and suffers dishonor if one female member fails to maintain the value of female chastity."[5] After her thorough description of the role and importance of virginity and chastity, Torjesen offers an example of female suicide in response to being raped.[6] She does not, however, provide an analysis of honor killing.

Why do some modern interpreters of the Bible identify the importance of female virginity and chastity in the New Testament world but do not consider the possibility of honor killings? Is the practice of honor kill-

---

this possibility when interpreting Matthew 1:19. See Malina and Rohrbaugh, *Social-Science Commentary on the Synoptic Gospels*, 26.

3. Osiek and MacDonald, *A Woman's Place*, 9.

4. Torjesen, *When Women Were Priests*, 137–138.

5. Ibid., 140.

6. Torjesen describes the suicide of Lucretia (as told by Livy). Suicide was her response to being raped. This story will be dealt with in greater detail below.

ing an ancient act? According to modern Palestinians and experts in ancient Middle Eastern history, the practice of honor killing is centuries old. Further, the practice is described as deeply embedded in patriarchal culture. For example, Suzanne Ruggi, a staff reporter for *The Jerusalem Times*, emphasizes that honor killing emerged in the pre-Islamic era. Furthermore, this practice stemmed from the patriarchal and patrilineal society's interest in maintaining strict control over family power structures. In Ruggi's interview with Sarif Kanaana, professor of anthropology at Birzeit University, Kanaana noted that honor killings are "a complicated issue that cuts deep into the history of Arab society."[7] In his article, "Reputation is Everything: Honor Killing Among the Palestinians," James Emory also emphasizes that the murder of females in the name of honor is an ancient tradition in the Middle East. Similar to Ruggi and Kanaana, Emory emphasizes that honor killings occurred prior to the arrival of Islam in 622 CE and that it is not a "religious" or "Islamic" practice, but has deep roots in the culture of Palestine. Finally, M. Aslam Khaki, in describing the history of honor killings in Pakistan, explains that, "The history of honor killings seems as old as man himself."[8] His justification for this claim is found in the relationship between honor killings and male control over female chastity in both ancient and modern patriarchal cultures. According to Khaki, it is a feeling of possessiveness, coupled with a sense of "moral duty" to defend a loss of honor that was, and continues to be, the cause of honor killings.[9]

While it is possible to consult many more modern Middle Eastern writers regarding the ancient roots of honor killings, the focus of this chapter is to show that ancient texts themselves testify to the practice. In other words, it is not enough to talk about the history of honor killings. We must also find evidence of the practice in the various writings from the ancient world. Therefore, I will turn now to a variety of ancient Mediterranean voices. In the end, we will find that the violence of honor killings is indeed both modern and ancient.

7. Ruggi, "Honor Killings in Palestine," 13.

8. Khaki, *Honour, Killings in Pakistan & Islamic View*, 3. Dr. Khaki's official titles include Juris-Consultant Federal Shariat Court and Advocate Supreme Court of Pakistan.

9. Khaki also notes that in Pakistan, a lack of education, low socioeconomic background and possible ulterior motives may also be causes for honor killings. See ibid., 8.

False Accusations and Honor Killing in
the Book of Susanna

The apocryphal book of Susanna (the 13th chapter of the Greek version of Daniel) is an appropriate place to begin our discussion of the ancient practice of honor killings. In this story, a rich man, Joakim, is married to the very beautiful Susanna. Joakim's house has a large garden and the Judeans often visit his house because he is honorable. Among the visitors are two elders who have been appointed as judges. The elders are frequently at Joakim's house and all who have a case to be tried come to them there. As time passes, both elders begin to lust for Susanna. Day after day, they wait eagerly to see her. On one particularly hot day, Susanna decides to bathe outdoors, in the garden. The elders wait and watch as Susanna is left alone and the garden doors are closed. Once they are alone with Susanna, the elders make their presence and their lustful intentions known.

According to Susanna 19–22, Susanna is presented with a dilemma. She will either be raped by the elders or be falsely accused of adultery. In either case, she will be killed.

> When the maids had gone out, the two elders got up and ran to her. They said, "Look, the garden doors are shut, and no one can see us. We are burning with desire for you; so give your consent, and lie with us. If you refuse, we will testify against you that a young man was with you, and this was why you sent your maids away." Susanna groaned and said, "I am completely trapped. For if I do this, it will mean death for me; if I do not, I cannot escape your hands. I choose not to do it; I will fall into your hands, rather than sin in the sight of the Lord."

In other words, if Susanna does commit adultery, she will be killed. On the other hand, if she does not lie with the men, she will be falsely accused of adultery. This, too, will lead to her death. Since she is faced with a death sentence either way, she refuses the men and plans to die because of the false accusations of the elders. At least this way, she did not actually commit the sin of adultery in the sight of the Lord.

The next day, as people gather at the house of Joakim, the elders come, plotting to have Susanna put to death. As the people listen, the elders falsely accuse Susanna of adultery.

> "While we were walking in the garden alone, this woman came in with two maids, shut the garden doors, and dismissed the maids.

42

Then a young man, who was hiding there, came to her and lay with her. We were in a corner of the garden, and when we saw this wickedness we ran to them. Although we saw them embracing, we could not hold the man, because he was stronger than we are, and he opened the doors and got away. We did, however, seize this woman and asked who the young man was, but she would not tell us. These things we testify." (Susanna 36–41)

After hearing the accusation, the assembly of Judeans accepts the false testimony of the elders and condemns Susanna to death. It is important to note that this story does not describe a formal trial, but rather emphasizes the community's role in determining the winner and loser in an honor contest. In this case, the community has determined that Susanna's actions have brought shame to the house of Joakim. In response, Susanna must be killed.

The story concludes with Susanna's innocence and life restored. She cries out to the Lord and the wickedness and lies of the elders are exposed, however, not before revealing an important dynamic of ancient Judean culture. In this story, the elders, Susanna (and presumably Joakim), and the Judean assembly all assume that if Susanna has committed adultery she will be killed. Importantly, this story also reveals that an honor killing may occur even if there is no "proof" of adultery. In this case a false accusation is enough to sentence a woman to death.[10]

Defiling the Name of the Father's House: Honor Killing in *Jubilees*

Two early examples of the discussion of honor killings are found in the Old Testament Pseudepigrapha, namely, the book of *Jubilees* (sometimes called the "Lesser Genesis").[11] *Jubilees* was written in Hebrew around 150 BCE and retells the story of Genesis 1 through Exodus 20 as they were understood by the author. The book was well known to early Christian writers and reveals the assumption that the punishment for bringing shame to a

10. Bruce M. Metzger explains that that in one of his sermons on Susanna, John Chrysostom (c. 347–c. 407) emphasized her steadfast chastity and her fidelity to her marriage vows when facing death and family shame. Metzger, *An Introduction to the Apocrypha*, 112.

11. *Jubilees* is a canonical text in the Ethiopian Orthodox Church.

father's house through inappropriate sexual activity is death. The beginning of *Jubilees* 20 provides a description of such a violent punishment. In this section, Abraham offers a farewell testimony to his children. Here, he commands his children in righteous behavior. He notes that the family is to "set aside from among us all fornication and pollution. And when any woman or girl fornicates among you, you will burn her with fire . . ." (*Jub.* 20:4). In this story, it is clear that a woman or girl's sexual purity is directly related to family honor. In a case in which a woman or girl's action brings shame upon the family, she will be killed.

Similarly, in *Jub.* 30:7–8, the author discusses the law prohibiting marriage with foreigners. It is deemed shameful for a man to give his daughter or sister in marriage to a non-Judean. If this occurs, surely the man is to be killed. Important for this book, however, is the next declaration. The author of *Jubilees* explains that since the woman is understood to have brought shame to the father's house, her shameful action also warrants death.

> And if there is any man in Israel who wishes to give his daughter or his sister to any man who is from the seed of the gentiles, let him surely die, and let him be stoned because he has caused shame in Israel. And also the woman will be burned with fire because she has defiled the name of her father's house and so she will be uprooted from Israel.

This example, as with the previous example, reveals the assumption that a woman or girl's virginity is connected to her family's honor. More importantly, if her actions bring shame to her father's house, she is to be killed.

The Rape of the Levite's concubine and Honor Killing in Judges

A violent and gruesome story of abuse and gang rape is told in Judges. In the story, a Levite and his concubine are traveling from Bethlehem in Judah to the remote parts of the hill country of Ephraim. Along the way, they are shown hospitality by a man in the city of Gibeah. In the evening, the men of the city surround the house and start to pound on the door. They say to the old man, "Bring out the man who came into your house, so that we may have intercourse with him" (Judg 19:22).[12] The host objects and offers

12. This story is an echo of the Genesis story of Sodom and Gomorrah (Genesis 19:1–29). However, this story does not offer divine intervention to protect the concubine.

his virgin daughter and the man's concubine in his place. The men seize the concubine and rape her and abuse her throughout the night until the morning. In the morning, the concubine returns to the home of her host and falls at his door.

> In the morning her master got up, opened the door of the house, and when he went out to go on his way, there was his concubine lying at the door of the house, with her hands on the threshold. "Get up," he said to her, "we are going." But there was no answer. Then he put her on the donkey; and the man set out for his home. When he had entered his house, he took a knife, and grasping his concubine he cut her into twelve pieces, limb by limb, and sent her throughout the territory of Israel. Then he commanded the men who he sent, saying, "Thus shall you say to all the Israelites, 'Has such a thing ever happened since the day that the Israelites came up from the land of Egypt until this day? Consider it, take counsel, and speak out.'" (Judg 19:27–30)

The brutality of the men of the city is without question. The concubine is raped and abused throughout the night. However, the response of the Levite is also an act of extreme violence. The story never states that the concubine is found dead in the morning. We are told that she does not answer the Levite, but we are left with uncertainty regarding her welfare.[13] What is clear is the response of the Levite. The concubine is cut into twelve pieces, limb by limb.[14]

Therefore, the men of this city surpass the evil deeds of the residents of Sodom. For an explanation of the relationship between the stories, see Olson, "The Book of Judges," 877.

13. For an example of an interpreter who assumes that the concubine is alive, see Matthews, *Judges and Ruth*, 190. Matthew's writes, "Seeing that she is unable to respond, he casually ties her body to his donkey and returns to his house. He has no sympathy for her condition. What empathy there is for her suffering must be evoked by the reader." For examples of interpreters who emphasize that it is not known if the concubine is dead or alive, see McCann, *Judges*, 130–31; and Olson, "The Book of Judges," 877–78. For an example of an interpreter that assumes that the concubine is dead, see Boling, *Judges*, 276.

14. There is debate over the significance of this action. For example, Robert G. Boling explains that this action is, "Evidence for the pre-Israelite and non-Israelite use of a twelve-piece sacrifice for ritual healing . . ." (Boling, *Judges*, 276). In contrast, Dennis T. Olson explains that the action is a "grisly call to arms. His act is a morbid and twisted adaptation of a customary means of calling up an emergency military force in the ancient Near East" (Olson, "The Book of Judges," 878).

This story is certainly complex and I do not wish to oversimplify what are significant issues. For example, the actions take place in an Israelite society that is in chaos. Furthermore, the declaration of the Levite seems to indicate that he is horrified at the actions of the men (Has anything this terrible happed to us since our flight from Egypt?). We may, however, draw some important conclusions from this story. The Levite offers no sign of concern or mercy toward the concubine. He is able to sleep through the night while she is being abused and raped. Upon seeing her body on the doorstep, he simply commands her to, "get up." Finally, and most importantly, the mutilation of the concubine's body is intended to send a message to all of Israel. Is this a public declaration of the defense of family honor? While the story does present a number of questions, we may observe that modern honor killings continue to echo this ancient story. It is not only adultery that is punished with death, honor killings were, and continue to be, used to restore family honor in cases of abuse and rape.[15]

Adultery and Honor Killing in the Gospel of John

While the previous examples are found in the Apocrypha, the Old Testament Pseudepigrapha, and the Old Testament, an example of the assumption of an honor killing is also present in the New Testament. John 8:1–11 is the story of a woman who has been caught in adultery. In the story, Jesus is sitting and teaching at the Temple in Jerusalem. A number of scribes and Pharisees bring the adulterer and place her in the midst of the group that is gathered around Jesus. Challenging Jesus, they ask, "Teacher, this woman was caught in the very act of committing adultery. Now in the law Moses commanded to us to stone such women. Now what do you say?" (vv. 4–5). An essential detail of this story is that this not a formal trial. Rather, this story is based upon a *double* honor challenge.[16] The scribes and Pharisees

15. J. Clinton McCann warns that, "Reducing the social dynamic in Judges 19 to males victimizing females is problematic, because this dichotomy is itself a patriarchal way of thinking." He further stresses that while women are victimized in this chapter, they are more than victims as well. Furthermore, this story reflects an Israelite society that was in chaos. McCann, *Judges*, 132.

16. Bruce J. Malina and Richard L. Rohrbaugh note that, "there can be no doubt that this is a challenge to Jesus' honor, since his opponents' purpose is 'to test him' (v. 6)— that is, test his loyalty to God" (*Social-Science Commentary on the Gospel of John*, 293). Malina and Rohrbaugh also identify the dual nature of this honor challenge, although

challenge the honor of Jesus by asking him to interpret the law of Moses. Furthermore, they assume that the act of adultery is shameful, detrimental to family honor, and deserving of death. Will Jesus defend his honor by answering the challenge? Will Jesus uphold the ancient assumptions of honor and shame, of chastity and death, and sentence this woman to be stoned?

The scribes and Pharisees continue to question Jesus. After a time, Jesus says to the group, "Let anyone among you who is without sin be the first to throw a stone at her" (v. 7). After this response, the group goes away one by one, beginning with the elders. When Jesus is left alone with the woman, he says, "Woman, where are they? Has no one condemned you?" (v. 10). The woman replies, "No one, sir." Finally, he proclaims, "Neither do I condemn you. Go your way, and from now on do not sin again" (v. 11).

In this story, Jesus responds to both challenges. First, Jesus defends his honor through a response in the form of a corresponding challenge to the scribes and Pharisees. It is they, not he, who are shamed, for not one is found to be free from sin. Second, Jesus responds to the ancient assumptions of adultery and death. While Jesus does acknowledge the sin, he challenges the assumption that such an act should be punishable by death. Important for the present discussion is the assumption held by the scribes and Pharisees (and presumably by the group gathered around Jesus), that adultery is, and ought to be, punishable by death.

Honor Killing in Greco-Roman Literature

It is not only in biblical literature that we find evidence of ancient honor killings. In fact, throughout classical literature we find the relationship between a girl's virginity and family honor, as well as the assumption that an honor killing is the appropriate punishment for adultery. In her text, *Goddesses, Whores, Wives, and Slaves*, Susan B. Pomeroy describes the result of adultery in the Roman world: "Augustus declared adultery a public offense only in women. Consistent with the power of the *pater familias*, the father of the adulteress was permitted to kill her if she had not been

---

their description is different than mine. They conclude that "Jesus' opponents use the woman's loss of her shame to ensnare Jesus' honor" (*Social-Science Commentary on the Gospel of John*, 293).

emancipated from his power."[17] This permission to kill is based upon the loss of family honor due to the shameful act of the woman.

The assumption of honor killings, however, predates the declaration of Augustus. Mary R. Lefkowitz and Maureen B. Fant offer an excerpt from a speech called *On the Dowry* by the Roman statesman, Marcus Cato (234–149 BCE). In this speech, Cato describes the right of the husband to kill a wife caught committing adultery.

> The husband . . . who divorces his wife is her judge, as though he were a censor; he has power if she has done something perverse and awful; if she has drunk wine she is punished; if she has done wrong with another man, she is condemned to death. It is written regarding the right to kill: "If you catch your wife in adultery, you can kill her with impunity; she, however, cannot dare to lay a finger on you if you commit adultery, nor is it the law."[18]

Here, Cato the Elder highlights not only the double-standard regarding adultery in the ancient world, but describes the punishment for a woman caught in adultery. In this case, the practice of honor killing is understood in terms of the "right" of the man.

The Roman writer and historian, Livy, also recognizes the assumption of honor killings at the turn of the first-century. Writing during the reign of Augustus, Livy tells the story of Sextus Tarquinius, the son of the last great king of Rome, and his rape of Lucretia.

> Sextus Tarquinius . . . was brought after dinner to a guest-chamber. Burning with passion, he waited till it seemed to him that all about him was secure and everybody fast asleep; then, drawing his sword, he came to the sleeping Lucretia. Holding the woman down with his left hand on her breast, he said, "Be still, Lucretia! I am Sextus Tarquinius. My sword is in my hand. Utter a sound and you die!" In affright the woman started out of her sleep. No help was in sight, but only imminent death. Then Tarquinius began to declare his love, to plead, to mingle threats with prayers, to bring every resource to bear upon her woman's heart. When he found her obdurate and not to be moved even by fear of death, he went farther and threatened

---

17. Pomeroy, *Goddesses, Whores, Wives, and Slaves*, 159. Pomeroy cites *Digest* 48.5.21 (Papinian, *On Adultery*, Book 1). "The right is granted to the father to kill an adulterer with a daughter while she is under his power. Therefore no other relative can legally do this, nor can a son in paternal power, who is a father."

18. Lefkowitz and Fant, *Women's Life in Greece and Rome*, 97.

her with disgrace, saying that when she was dead he would kill his slave and lay him naked by her side, that she might be said to have been put to death in adultery with a man of base condition. At this dreadful prospect her resolute modesty was overcome, as if with force, by his victorious lust; and Tarquinius departed, exulted in his conquest of a woman's honour.[19]

In this terrible story of violence and rape, Livy reveals with profound power the reality of honor killings in the ancient world. Lucretia resisted the pleading of Tarquinius. Further, Lucretia resisted the death threats of Tarquinius. However, the thought of lying dead next to a man of "base condition" with the community thinking that she had been killed in defense of honor because of adultery, Lucretia gives in to the rape. In other words, the fear of being thought the victim of an honor killing was worse than the reality of being forcefully and violently raped.

The end of the story is as difficult and tragic as the beginning. Lucretia sent word of her rape to her family. Surprisingly, her father and husband sought "to comfort her, sick at heart as she is, by diverting the blame from her who was forced to the doer of the wrong. They tell her it is the mind that sins, not the body; and that where purpose has been wanting there is no guilt."[20] Lucretia, however, understands the punishment for adultery.

"It is up to you to determine," she answers, "what is due to him; for my own part, though I acquit myself of the sin, I do not absolve myself from punishment; not in time to come shall ever unchaste woman live through the example of Lucretia." Taking a knife which she had concealed beneath her dress, she plunged it into her heart, and sinking forward upon the wound, died as she fell. The wail of the dead was raised by her husband and her father.[21]

While some may wish to focus upon the gracious response of her father and husband, Livy emphasizes the assumed punishment for adultery. Never will a woman be allowed to commit adultery and use Lucretia as an "excuse" to avoid the appropriate punishment.

Livy also tells the story of Appius Claudius who was seized by desire and lust to debauch Verginia.[22] In his introduction to the story, he makes

19. Livy 1.58.1–5.
20. Livy 1.58.9–10.
21. Livy 1.58.10–12.
22. Livy 3.44.

a direct connection to his earlier telling of the story of Lucretia. Livy notes that an outrage happened in Rome "which was inspired by lust and was no less shocking in its consequences than that which had led, through rape and the death of Lucretia . . ."[23] The story of Appius Claudius and Verginia ends with the girl being murdered by her father that she may never have her chastity threatened. The killing of his daughter, the father reasoned, was the only way that he could uphold and insure her freedom. While the story does not deal directly with honor killings, it forcefully highlights the importance of female chastity and its relationship with family honor. Furthermore, this story highlights that murder is understood to be appropriate when a woman's virginity (and a family's honor) is at risk.

Another example of honor killing in the ancient Mediterranean world is found in the writing of Suetonius. In his work on the life of Augustus, he describes the shame brought upon Augustus' family by the sexual activity of his daughter, Julia, and his granddaughter, also named Julia.

> But at the height of his happiness and his confidence in his family and its training, Fortune proved fickle. He found the two Julias, his daughter and granddaughter, guilty of every form of vice, and banished them . . . he informed the senate of his daughter's fall through a letter read in his absence by a quaestor, and for very shame would meet no one for a long time, and even thought of putting her to death. At all events, when one of her confidantes, a freedwoman called Phoebe, hanged herself at about the same time, he said, "I would rather have been Phoebe's father."[24]

Besides the shame brought upon the family of Augustus through the sexual activity of the two Julias, Augustus also found great displeasure with his adopted third grandson, Agrippa. Agrippa is described as being a man of low tastes and violent temper. Very tellingly, Suetonius explains the extent of the shame brought upon the family by the actions of Agrippa and the two Julias: "at every mention of him and of the Julias he would sigh deeply and even cry out: 'Would that I ne'er had wedded and would I had died without offspring'; and he never alluded to them except as his three boils and his three ulcers."[25] While Augustus considers the honor killing of his daughter, he finally settles upon her banishment from Rome. This punishment, how-

---

23. Livy 3.44.1.
24. Suetonius, *Augustus* 65.1–3.
25. Suetonius, *Augustus* 65.4.

ever, does not diminish the shame felt by Augustus. He refuses to meet with people due to his shame and even admires the father of a suicide victim. His reference to his daughter as a boil and an ulcer proves beyond dispute the relationship between female sexual purity and family honor, and his very real consideration of the honor killing of Julia.

Honor Killing in Ancient Jewish Literature

The assumption that death is the appropriate penalty for adultery is also present in ancient Jewish literature. For example, in his description of the adultery of David and Bathsheeba, the first-century historian, Josephus notes that when she became pregnant there was a need to contrive some way to conceal her sin—for, according to the laws of the fathers, she was deserving of death as an adulteress.[26] Throughout his writing, Josephus indicates that honor killings were not simply theoretical, but were also a matter of practice. For example, Josephus reports that King Herod's sister's *husband* had been put to death on a charge of adultery.[27] As we might expect in first-century literature, while a "high-profile" male honor killing is documented, the murder of "common" girls and women in defense of family honor remain untold.

While the relationship between adultery and family honor is apparent in the writing of Josephus, it is a reoccurring theme in the writing of the Jewish historian and philosopher, Philo. According to Philo, adultery is the greatest of all crimes.[28] He notes that it is natural that "the abominable and God-detested sin of adultery was placed first in the list of wrongdoing."[29] Several reasons are provided to justify this claim, not the least of which is the damage done to family honor:

> Indeed it makes havoc of three families; of that of the husband who suffers from the breach of faith, stripped of the promise of his marriage-vows and his hopes of legitimate offspring, and of two others, those of the adulterer and the woman, for the infec-

---

26. Josephus, *Jewish Antiquities* 7.131.
27. Josephus, *Jewish War* 1.486.
28. Philo, *On the Decalogue* 121–31.
29. Philo, *On the Decalogue* 131.

tion of the outrage and dishonour and disgrace of the deepest kind extends to the family of both.[30]

Philo does not stop with a discussion of the damage done to family honor through adultery, he forcefully and repeatedly explains that the proper punishment for adultery is death. For example, in describing a woman suspected of adultery, he notes that she is threatened by two dangers. First, she is in danger of losing her life. Second, she is in danger of bringing shame on her past. He notes that the latter danger is a far more grievous thing than death.[31] In fact, time and time again, Philo notes that death is the proper punishment for adulterers.[32]

While Philo clearly explains that an honor killing is the appropriate punishment for an adulterous woman, he goes to much greater lengths to insist that the punishment for males is also death. In discussing the punishment for males caught in the most heinous crime of adultery, he notes that "the proper punishment for him is death and for the woman also."[33] He further notes that the soul of the male adulterer is incurably diseased and that "such persons must be punished with death."[34]

Perhaps Philo's most forceful defense of death as the proper punishment for adulterous males is found in his description of the Old Testament figure, Joseph. As Joseph was winning a high reputation in household affairs in Egypt, his master's wife made him the object of her desires. Joseph responds to her with am an impassioned speech:

> The end we seek in wedlock is not pleasure but the begetting of lawful children. To this day I have remained pure, and I will not take the first step in transgression by committing adultery, the greatest of crimes. For even if I had always hitherto lived an irregular life, drawn by the appetites of youth and following after the luxury of this land, I ought not to make the wedded wife of another my prey. Who does not thirst for the blood of the adulterer? For while men are accustomed to differ on other matters they are all and everywhere of one mind on this; they count the culprits wor-

30. Philo, *On the Decalogue* 126.
31. Philo, *On the Special Laws*, 3.52–53.
32. See Philo, *On the Special Laws* 3.58, 72–73; and Philo, *Hypothetica* 7.1.
33. Philo, *On the Special Laws* 3.31.
34. Philo, *On the Special Laws* 3.11.

thy of a multitude of deaths, and deliver them unjudged into the hands of those who have discovered their guilt.[35]

With these words placed into the mouth of Joseph, Philo describes his understanding of the appropriate punishment for adultery. It is important to note that Philo emphasizes the punishment for *men* caught in adultery only because for him the punishment for women needs little or no defense or explanation. When a woman has shamed her family through inappropriate sexual behavior, the punishment is also death.

In addition, the discussion of honor killing is present in the Mishnah (ca. 200 CE). According to *Sanhedrin* 7.9, "He that has connexion [*sic*] with a girl that is betrothed is not culpable unless she is still in her girlhood, and a virgin, and betrothed, and still in her father's house. If two had connexion with her the first is [liable to death] by stoning, but the second [only] by strangling."[36] Similarly, *Sanhedrin* 9.1 details those adulterers who are to be burnt.[37] While historians have long debated whether or not the Mishnah reflects the actions and practice of first-century Judeans, at the very least the discussion of death as the punishment for adultery again supports that the practice of honor killings is ancient.

Adultery as Metaphor and Metaphorical Honor Killing in the Old Testament Prophets

The relationship between adultery, family honor, and honor killing is also present in the speeches of Old Testament prophets. For example, the prophet Hosea describes the infidelity of Israel in terms of adultery and explains that the penalty for such metaphorical adultery is death (Hos 2:2–3). Similarly, the prophet Ezekiel describes the punishment for Jerusalem's infidelity in terms of adultery. The penalty for this act is brutal and graphic, leading to stripping, stoning, and cutting the offending body to pieces:

> Therefore, O whore, hear the word of the LORD: Thus says the Lord GOD, Because your lust was poured out and your nakedness uncovered in your whoring with your lovers, and because of all your abominable idols, and because of the blood of your children

35. Philo, *On Joseph*, 43–44.
36. *Sanhedrin* 7.9. See Danby, *Mishnah*, 393.
37. *Sanhedrin* 9.1. See Danby, *Mishnah*, 395.

that you gave to them, therefore, I will gather all your lovers, with whom you took pleasure, all those you loved and all those you hated; I will gather them against you from all around, and will uncover your nakedness to them, so that they may see all your nakedness. I will judge you as women who commit adultery and shed blood are judged, and bring blood upon you in wrath and jealousy. I will deliver you into their hands, and they shall throw down your platform and break down your lofty places; they shall strip you of your clothes and take your beautiful objects and leave you naked and bare. They shall bring up a mob against you, and they shall stone you and cut you to pieces with their swords. They shall burn your houses and execute judgments on you in the sight of many women; I will stop you from playing the whore, and you shall also make no more payments. So I will satisfy my fury on you, and my jealousy shall turn away from you; I will be calm, and will be angry no longer. Because you have not remembered the days of your youth, but have enraged me with all these things; therefore, I have returned your deeds upon your head, says the Lord God (Ezekiel 16:35–43)

While Ezekiel's description of the adultery of Israel is metaphorical, it is striking that the appropriate punishment for such shameful actions is still described in terms of honor killing. In short, the prophet's words reveal a profound truth about ancient Judea: when actions are described in terms of adultery, the severity of the punishment is understood.

Early Christian Interpretations of the Birth Narrative in Matthew

How did early Christians understand Joseph's dilemma? Did they, as modern interpreters do, assume that Joseph's dilemma involved the decision between public or private divorce? Or, did early Christians assume that Joseph's dilemma included the very real possibility that Mary might be killed? To better understand how early Christians interpreted the context of the birth narrative in Matthew, it is helpful to explore *The Protevangelium of James*.[38] This "proto-gospel" was written in the latter half of the second-

38. For a Greek and English version of the *Protevangelium of James*, see Hock, *The Infancy Gospels of James and Thomas*, 32–76. For an alternate Greek text, see Smid, *Protevangelium Jacobi*, 25–171. For an additional description and translation of the

century[39] and was very popular for hundreds of years. J. K. Elliot summarizes the origin and impact of this text:

> The text, which was probably originally composed in the second century, was particularly popular in the East. Over 150 manuscripts of it in Greek have survived. These dated from several centuries, thus indicating its long-standing popularity. It was translated into several early versions (Coptic, Syriac, Georgian, Armenian, Ethiopian, and Slavonic) showing that it was also popular in a wide geographical area. Latin versions also exist, albeit not in great numbers.[40]

While the text is referred to as an "infancy-gospel," it actually tells the story of two important births. The story begins with the birth of Mary and tells of her childhood and her betrothal to Joseph.[41] The gospel also tells the story of the birth of Jesus and extends through Herod's killing of the infant boys. Most important for this book, however, is that the text builds upon the Gospel of Matthew. In other words, the author of the *Protevangelium of James* attempts to fill in the gaps in Matthew's gospel. He attempts to provide a more detailed picture of the birth of Jesus than that which is found in

---

Protevangelium of James, see Schneemelcher, *New Testament Apocrypha*, 421–39. For an alternate English translation of the *Protevangelium of James*, see Elliott, *The Apocryphal New Testament*, 48–67. For a brief introduction to the *Protevangelium of James*, see Ehrman, *After the New Testament*, 247–48.

39. See Hock, *The Infancy Gospel of James and Thomas* 11. Hock explains, "To be sure, dates for the Infancy Gospel of James have ranged widely over the years—from the mid-second century to as late as the fifth. The later end of this range was proposed by scholars at the beginning of this century, but the earlier centuries are preferred by scholars today." Because the contexts of the Protevangelium of James do not provide any indication about the time that it was written, historians must rely upon external evidence. In so doing, it is widely held that the proto-gospel must have been written sometime during the second half of the second century. For a study of the external evidence commonly used in the dating of the *Protevangelium of James*, see Smid, *Protevangelium Jacobi*, 22–24.

40. Elliott, *A Synopsis of the Apocryphal Nativity and Infancy Narratives*, xii–xiii. See also Horner, "Jewish Aspects of the Protoevangelium of James," 313–35.

41. J. K. Elliot explains that this text also reflects the developing tradition of the perpetual virginity of Mary. He explains, "Its stories reflect the developing tradition that was ultimately expressed in the Christian dogma on the perpetual virginity of Mary. In addition it gave support and impetus to feasts such as the Immaculate Conception of Mary and the Presentation in the Temple" (Elliott, *A Synopsis of the Apocryphal Nativity and Infancy Narratives*, xii).

the canonical gospel of Matthew. Ronald F. Hock explains the relationship between the Infancy Gospel of James and the Gospel of Matthew:

> The Infancy Gospel of James . . . extends the canonical birth stories back to the circumstances surrounding the birth of Mary and her childhood and ends shortly after the birth of Jesus with its own version of Matthew's account of the murder of the infants. But this dependence on Matthew's account is not the only instance. In fact, the Infancy Gospel of James assumes, reworks, and develops both Matthew's and Luke's stories at many points throughout the narrative.[42]

For most interpreters of the *Protevangelium of James*, the gospel appears to be more interested in the birth and life of Mary than that of Jesus. J. Ed Kosmoszewski, M. James Sawyer, and Daniel B. Wallace provide a helpful summary of this position:

> The Protevangelium of James is more about Mary, the mother of Jesus, than about Jesus. It is unashamedly a work intended to glorify her. As perhaps the earliest infancy gospel, it shows more restraint than later gospels. But there are still remarkable incidents in the life of Mary and Jesus that go beyond the conservative descriptions found in the canonical Gospels. For example, Mary is dedicated to the temple at a young age; she was "nurtured like a dove and received food from the hand of an angel" until she was twelve years old. The Protevangelium of James expands on the infancy narratives in the Gospel of Matthew and Luke, filling in details with vivid imagination. It obviously is based on Matthew and Luke but adds much more entertaining material.[43]

While the author does focus a great deal of attention on Mary, he also reveals an important assumption regarding Joseph's dilemma. Joseph's dilemma is not that of public versus private divorce, but was indeed that of the possible honor killing of Mary. Joseph reasons that if he does not reveal Mary's pregnancy, he will be going against the law of the Lord. However, if he does reveal Mary's pregnancy, he will be handing her over to a death sentence.

---

42. Hock, *The Infancy Gospels of James and Thomas*, 4–5. For further examples of how the author presupposes and makes free use of the Gospel of Matthew, see Schneemelcher, *New Testament Apocrypha*, 423. See also Kosmoszewski, Sawyer, and Wallace, *Reinventing Jesus*, 154–55.

43. Kosmoszewski, Sawyer, and Wallace, *Reinventing Jesus*, 154–55.

(13:1) She was in her sixth month when one day Joseph came home from his building projects, entered his house, and found her pregnant. (13:2) He struck himself in the face, threw himself to the ground on sackcloth, and began to cry bitterly; "What sort of face should I present to the Lord God? (13:3)What prayer can I say on her behalf since I received her as a virgin from the temple of the Lord God and didn't protect her? (13:4) Who has set this trap for me? Who has done this evil deed in my house? Who has lured this virgin away from me and violated her? (13:5) The story of Adam has been repeated in my case hasn't it? For just as Adam was praying when the serpent came and found Eve alone, deceived her, and corrupted her, so the same thing has happened to me." (13:6) So Joseph got up from the sackcloth and summoned Mary and said to her, "God has taken a special interest in you – how could you have done this? (13:7) Have you forgotten the Lord your God? Why have you brought shame on yourself, you who were raised in the Holy of Holies and fed by a heavenly messenger?" (13:8) But she began to cry bitter tears: "I'm innocent. I haven't had sex with any man." (13:9) And Joseph said to her, "Then where did the child you're carrying come from?" (13:10) And she replied, "As the Lord my God lives, I don't know where it came from."

(14:1) And Joseph became very frightened and no longer spoke with her as he pondered what he was going to do with her. (14:2) And Joseph said to himself, "If I try to cover up her sin, I'll end up going against the law of the Lord. (14:3) And if I disclose her condition to the people of Israel, I'm afraid that the child inside her might be heaven-sent and I'll end up handing innocent blood over to a death sentence. (14:4) So what should I do with her? [I know,] I'll divorce her quietly." (14:5) But when night came a messenger of the Lord suddenly appeared to him in a dream and said: "Don't be afraid of this girl, because the child in her is the holy spirit's doing. (14:6) She will have a son and you will name him Jesus—the name means 'he will save his people from their sins.'" (14:7) And Joseph got up from his sleep and praised the God of Israel, who had given him this favor (14:8). And so he began to protect the girl.[44]

In this short section, the author of the proto-gospel of James reveals three important assumptions regarding Joseph's dilemma. First, Joseph assumes that Mary has committed adultery. Second, neither Joseph nor Mary know from where (or whom) the child has come. Third, Joseph assumes

44. Hock, *The Infancy Gospels of James and Thomas*, 55–59.

that if Mary's adultery and subsequent pregnancy is made known, she will be killed. In other words, this text reveals with clarity and certainty that early Christians understood Joseph's dilemma to be that of the possible honor killing of Mary.

Ronald F. Hock provides a recent and thorough commentary on the *Infancy Gospel of James*. However, nowhere in his summary of the text or in his notes does he propose that Joseph's dilemma is that of an honor killing.[45] Hock explains, "Joseph is at a loss about what to do with her (14:1–3), and he even has thoughts of divorcing her quietly (14:4), thoughts which recall the situation in Matt 1:19. But a dream in which a heavenly messenger appears to him resolves his doubts."[46] It seems, in fact, that Hock jumps from 14:1 to 14:4 in his reading of the text, completely overlooking Joseph's actual dilemma. Again, we find that while modern readers are eager to discuss the possible divorce of Mary, there is no discussion of honor killing.

In an earlier commentary on the *Protevangelium of James*, H. R. Smid states that Joseph's dilemma is an elaboration of Matt 1:19.[47] Where Matt 1:19 reveals a dilemma for Joseph, the author of the proto-gospel of James explains the nature of the dilemma: if Mary's pregnancy is made known, she will be killed. With regard to the possible killing of Mary, Smid focuses very shortly on Deut 22:13–29, but does not deal with honor killings. Perhaps most significantly, Smid concludes that, "Perhaps one might term these words the core of [the Protevangelium of James]: innocent blood is saved."[48]

"Innocent blood is saved." Indeed, this phrase is the core of the *Protevangelium of James*. However, this phrase has yet to be used by modern readers in the context of honor killings. In this infancy gospel, a gospel that was popular over a wide geographical area for several centuries, we find a clear description of Joseph's dilemma. Joseph does not, as modern readers often propose, consider his choices to be that of public versus private divorce. Joseph does consider his dilemma to be that of silence (and subsequent disobedience to the law of the Lord) and making Mary's adultery known (and her subsequent honor killing). In short, while modern readers may struggle with the reality of honor killings in the ancient world,

---

45. See Hock, *The Infancy Gospel of James and Thomas*, 6 (summary) and 55 (notes).

46. Ibid., 6.

47. Smid, *Protevangelium Jacobi*, 99.

48. Ibid., 101.

this was precisely the context which was assumed by early Christians when considering Joseph's dilemma.

An early, anonymous Christian interpretation of Matt 1:19 echoes the *Protevangelium of James*. While little is known regarding the historical context of this work, the anonymous author does make clear that Joseph's dilemma is that of the honor killing of Mary.

> Perhaps Joseph thought within himself: If I should conceal her sin, I would be acting against God's law, and if I should publicize it to the sons of Israel, they would stone her. I fear that what is in her womb is of divine intervention. Didn't Sarah conceive when she was ninety years of age and bring forth a child? If God caused that woman who was like dry wood to flower, what if the Godhead wanted Mary to bear a child without the aid of a man? . . . What shall I do then? I will put her away secretly, because it is better in an uncertain matter that a known prostitute should get off free than that an innocent person should die. It is indeed more just that an unjust person should escape justly than that a just person should die unjustly. If a guilty person should escape once, he can die another time. But if an innocent person should die once, he cannot be brought back.[49]

This text differs from the proto-gospel of James in Joseph's consideration of the origin of Mary's pregnancy. Here, Joseph wonders whether it is God who is the cause of Mary's pregnancy. Ironically, the pregnancy is still described of as "a sin." Importantly, even though the author does not portray Joseph as suspecting Mary of adultery, his dilemma remains the same. Should Joseph reveal Mary's sin? Or, should Joseph publicize her sin to the sons of Israel? If her pregnancy is discovered, she will be the victim of an honor killing. Even Joseph's decision to conceal Mary's sin is clothed in the language of honor killing. Joseph will not publicize Mary's pregnancy, because even if she has sinned and is worthy of death, she will still die at some point, the appropriate fate for an adulterous woman.

The two previous examples of early Christian interpretations of Joseph's dilemma reveal that the honor killing of Mary served as the context for reading Matt 1:19. The writing of John Chrysostom (c. 347–c. 407) reveals the same assumption regarding Joseph's dilemma. In other words, the possibility that Mary would be killed served as the context for reading Matt

---

49. Migne, *Patrologiae Cursus Completus*, 56:633. For this translation, see Simonetti, *Matthew 1–13*, 15.

1:19 at least through the fourth century. Among his many works is a series of homilies on the Gospel of Matthew. In one of Chrysostom's sermons, he describes Joseph's dilemma:

> Do you not see here a man of exceptional self-restraint, freed from that most tyrannical passion, jealousy? What an explosive thing jealousy is, of which it was rightly spoken: "For the soul of her husband is full of jealousy. He will not spare in the day of vengeance."[50] And "jealousy is cruel as the grave."[51] And we too know of many that have chosen to give up their lives rather than fall under the suspicion of jealousy. But in this case it was not a matter of simple suspicion, as the burden of Mary's own womb entirely convicted her. Nevertheless Joseph was so free from the passion of jealousy as to be unwilling to cause distress to the Virgin, even in the slightest way. To keep Mary in his house appeared to be a transgression of the law, but to expose and bring her to trial would cause him to deliver her to die. He would do nothing of the sort. So Joseph determined to conduct himself now by a higher rule than the law. For now that grace was appearing, it would be fitting that many tokens of that exalted citizenship be expressed.[52]

In this section, Chrysostom begins with a moving description of the power of jealousy. Furthermore, if anyone had a right to be jealous, it was Joseph. Mary's pregnancy convicted her, and yet, Joseph was not jealous. He did, however, face a dilemma. Should Joseph keep Mary in his house (and subsequently transgress the law) or should Joseph expose Mary's pregnancy (and subsequently deliver her to die)? While Chrysostom seems to be emphasizing the virtue of Joseph, he also reveals his assumption regarding Joseph's dilemma. Again, Joseph is not faced with the choice between public and private divorce. Rather, Joseph is faced with silence or exposure, with disobedience to the law of the Lord or with the honor killing of Mary.

---

50. Prov 6:34 LXX.

51. Song 8:6 LXX.

52. Chrysostom, *Homilies on the Gospel of St. Matthew* 4.7. For this translation, see Simonetti, *Matthew 1–13*, 14–15.

Conclusion

M. Aslam Khaki noted, "The history of honor killings seems as old as man himself."[53] Indeed, the connection between adultery, family honor, and the killing of girls and women may be found in Susanna, Jubilees, Judges, the Gospel of John, and in both Classical and Jewish literature. Further, early Christians assumed that Joseph's dilemma involved an honor killing. While modern readers of the birth narrative in Matthew tend to assume that Joseph's dilemma involved the choice between a public and a private divorce, ancient readers of Matthew envisioned a very different scenario. For early Christians, Joseph's dilemma was between keeping Mary's pregnancy silent and being disobedient to the law of the Lord or exposing Mary's pregnancy and handing her over to be killed. The *Protevangelium of James* is perhaps the most revealing interpretation of Joseph's dilemma. Written less than a century after the Gospel of Matthew, this infancy gospel expands on the canonical birth story. The author of the *Protevangelium of James* provides a clear description of the nature of Joseph's dilemma. In short, Joseph's dilemma involved the possible honor killing of Mary.

53. Khaki, *Honour, Killings in Pakistan & Islamic View*, 3.

4

Rethinking "Joseph's Dilemma"

SO WHAT? THAT IS truly the most important question. In the first chapter, I described the practice of honor killings in the modern Middle East. Girls and woman are killed in defense of family honor. Their stories are told in poems and short stories. Their deaths are described in documentaries, in newspapers, and in journal articles. In the second chapter, I outlined various modern readings of the birth narrative in Matthew. While readers come to the text with different assumptions, most leave with the same conclusion: Joseph's dilemma involved a choice between a public or a private divorce of Mary. In the third chapter, I outlined the ancient practice of honor killings. While it is tempting to envision a time when adultery and murder were only metaphorical descriptions of disloyalty and punishment, this was not the case. The practice of honor killings is both ancient and modern. Women and girls were killed in the defense of family honor then as they are now. But there is more, not only were women and girls killed in name of honor, early Christians assumed that this was the context of Joseph's dilemma. Joseph's dilemma was not over a public or private divorce. Joseph agonized over what he should do. If he keeps Mary's pregnancy a secret, he will be disobedient to the law of the Lord. If he reveals Mary's pregnancy, he will be handing Mary over to death. What is a righteous man to do?

So what? We return to that question. Why is it so important to rethink Joseph's dilemma? Why is it so important to consider the honor killing of Mary when we read the birth narrative in Matthew? Certainly this disrupts the now traditional image of the birth of Jesus. "Silent night, holy night," is replaced by suspected adultery and expected death. However, when we consider the context of an honor killing, we are introduced to an important theme that runs through the entirety of the gospel. In the brief story of Joseph's dilemma, the author introduces the theme, *from expected death comes unexpected new life.*

The Birth of Jesus

FROM EXPECTED DEATH COMES UNEXPECTED NEW LIFE

In Matthew's gospel, the story of the birth of Jesus is short. In eight succinct verses we are led from the discovery of Mary's pregnancy to the naming of the baby (Matt 1:18-25). Like its brevity, the birth narrative is surprisingly simple, straightforward, and free of details. Mary and Joseph discover that she is pregnant. While the readers are told that the pregnancy is "from the Holy Spirit," this information is not made known to Joseph until later in the story. Upon learning of Mary's pregnancy, Joseph is faced with a dilemma. What is a righteous man to do? We are told that he is "unwilling to expose her to public disgrace" and, therefore, "plans to dismiss her quietly." After his decision has been made, an angel of the Lord appears to Joseph in a dream. Joseph is told that he should not fear to take Mary as his wife. It is at this point that it is revealed to Joseph that "the child conceived in her is from the Holy Spirit." When Joseph awakes from his sleep, he takes Mary as his wife. Mary bears a son, and Joseph names him Jesus.

Historians have long noted that what is most surprising about the birth narrative in Matthew is what it *doesn't* say. There is no mention of animals or shepherds. There isn't an "inn" or a journey to Bethlehem. There is no manger or swaddling clothes, and there is no mention of a choir of angels. In addition, not only does Mary not sing praises to God for the gift of the child, she does not speak. Unless this story is intentionally harmonized with the birth narrative in the Gospel of Luke, readers are likely to come to one conclusion—Jesus was born at home in Bethlehem.

While it is interesting to consider what is *not* in Matthew's account of the birth of Jesus, we must look carefully at what *is* included in the story. Stated simply, the story focuses upon Joseph's dilemma. The first of the eight verses sets the scene: Mary is pregnant (1:18). The last of the eight verses serves as a conclusion: Mary gives birth and they name the child Jesus (1:25). The remaining six verses deal with Joseph's dilemma and his subsequent encounter with an angel of the Lord in a dream. While it is most certainly true that the angel describes the significance of the child—he will save the people from their sins—the description of the significance of Jesus is offered in response to Joseph's dilemma. At the center of this story is a righteous man who is faced with the realization that his betrothed is pregnant.

From the attention that the author places on both Joseph's dilemma and the angel's reply, it appears it is this aspect of the story that is being emphasized. But why would the author emphasize the exchange between Joseph and the angel? As explained in chapter 2, most modern interpreters understand Joseph's dilemma to be a decision between the public or private divorce of Mary. Furthermore, it is commonly understood that Joseph decided to divorce Mary quietly so that she might not be shamed. While this reading seems reasonable to twenty-first century men and women in the North Atlantic, this seems to be at great odds with both the ancient practice of honor killing and with early Christian interpretations of the text. In the end, such modern readings miss the significance of the exchange between Joseph and the angel. For them, the angel urges Joseph not to divorce Mary because the child that is in her is great and is conceived from the Holy Spirit.

Early Christian audiences, in contrast, describe in great detail the power and significance of this exchange. Mary, it is assumed, has committed adultery. In ancient Palestine, girls who have committed adultery have shamed their family. In order to restore the family's honor, the girl must be killed. Joseph is described as being a "righteous man." But what does that mean? According to early Christian interpretations of Matthew, Joseph's dilemma is between silence and exposure. Joseph understands that if he exposes Mary's pregnancy, he will be handing her over to death. However, if he conceals Mary's pregnancy, he will be disobedient to the law of the Lord. Joseph is both a man of mercy and a man who is faithful to the law. What is a righteous man to do?

It is in the midst of this dilemma that the angel of the Lord appears to Joseph in a dream. Joseph must not let Mary be killed, for she has not committed adultery. Furthermore, Joseph must not let Mary be killed, for the child that is in her is conceived from the Holy Spirit and he will save the people from their sins. In other words, this is not a modern story of a quiet divorce. This is an ancient story in which the expected outcome is death. While the expected outcome is death, it is the unexpected that occurs—Joseph, Mary, and Jesus experience new life. Joseph takes Mary as his wife, she gives birth, and they name the child Jesus. This dramatic reversal of fortunes, from expected death to unexpected new life, serves as a theme that the author of Matthew emphasizes throughout this gospel. For us to miss this reversal, the reversal from death to life, is to miss the introduction of the theme altogether.

The Ministry of Jesus

FROM EXPECTED DEATH COMES UNEXPECTED NEW LIFE

The author of Matthew masterfully weaves this theme—from expected death comes unexpected new life—throughout the gospel. The story that immediately follows the birth of Jesus is that of the visit of the Magi (2:1–23). The men from the East visit Jerusalem and ask, "Where is the child who has been born king of the [Judeans]? For we observed his star at its rising, and have come to pay him homage." When Herod the king hears this question, he is deeply troubled. Certainly *he* is the king of Judea. Herod gathers the chief priests and the scribes and asks where Jesus is to be born. Upon hearing that the child is to be born in Bethlehem, he devises a plan. Herod summons the Magi and instructs them to search for the child and report back to him, that he, too, might worship this new king. Following the star, the Magi find the house and see the child with Mary his mother and they fall down and worship him. After giving the child gifts of gold, frankincense and myrrh, they are warned in a dream not to return to Herod. An angel of the Lord also appears to Joseph in a dream and announces that he is to take Mary and the child and flee to Egypt. They are to do this, for Herod is about to search for the child in order to kill him.

When Herod realizes that he has been tricked by the Magi, he is in a furious rage. He orders that every male child two years and under in Bethlehem and throughout the region be killed. The story does not report how many children are killed. It does, however, report the mourning and wailing and loud laments. As for Joseph, Mary, and the child, they remain in Egypt until the death of Herod. After his death, an angel of the Lord appears to Joseph and instructs him to return to the land of Israel.

Immediately after telling the story of the birth of Jesus, a story in which Mary and her unborn child face expected death, the author of Matthew tells another story of violence and murder. The story is dramatic and continues to capture the imaginations of all who hear the account. It is easy to imagine Herod's men searching for and killing all male infants. The story makes clear that this is a moment of expected death. However, just as an angel of the Lord visited Joseph in the midst of his dilemma, again an angel of the Lord visits Joseph in the midst of Herod's violent plan. Just as Mary and her unborn child were granted unexpected new life, Jesus is again spared and new life prevails.

Throughout his public ministry, the Gospel of Matthew paints a vivid picture of Jesus and his disciples traveling throughout Galilee. Jesus teaches and preaches and heals many. On one particular day, Jesus and his disciples get into a boat and a great windstorm arises on the sea (8:23–27). The storm is so great that waves begin to swamp the boat. While water threatens to overtake them, Jesus remains asleep. The author of Matthew describes the fear of the disciples who wake Jesus and beg, "Save us Lord, for we are perishing!" Jesus wakes from his sleep and questions the disciples. "Why are you afraid, you of little faith?" At that moment, Jesus gets up and rebukes the winds and the sea and there is a dead calm. At this, the disciples are amazed. They say to one another, "What sort of man is this, that even the winds and the sea obey him?" The author of Matthew again captures the attention of generations of listeners and readers. How is it that Jesus was able to sleep through such a storm? What must the disciples have felt as the water threatened to sink their boat? More importantly, the author again weaves into the narrative the theme that from expected death comes unexpected new life. Certainly the disciples believe that they are facing death. They plead with Jesus, "We are perishing!" But there is something different about this story. In the birth narrative and again in Herod's killing of the infants, it is Jesus who is saved. But in this story, it is Jesus who offers unexpected new life. The theme remains the same, from expected death comes unexpected new life, but now it is Jesus who is the actor, the agent of life.

The ministry of Jesus continues. He continues to call disciples and continues to teach. As Jesus is teaching, a leader of the synagogue comes to him and kneeling before him, says, "My daughter has just died; but come and lay your hand on her, and she will live" (9:18–26). Upon hearing this,

Jesus gets up and follows the man. The disciples of Jesus also follow. At this point in the story, the author weaves in another story of healing. A woman who has been hemorrhaging for twelve years touches the fringe of Jesus' cloak. He turns and announces to the woman, "Take heart, daughter, your faith has made you well." Instantly, the woman is restored to health and Jesus, his disciples, and the man continue along their way. Upon reaching the home, Jesus sees a crowd making a great commotion. He proclaims, "Go away; for the girl is not dead but sleeping." The crowd responds with laughter. This is not *expected* death, the girl is truly dead. Nonetheless, the crowd moves outside of the home and Jesus enters. He takes the girl by the hand and she gets up. The report of this event spreads quickly throughout the district. Just as Jesus grants new life to his disciples in the midst of a storm at sea, Jesus gives unexpected new life to a girl who has died.

In the Gospel of Matthew, the theme of expected death and unexpected new life is also used in relation to "social" death. In the first-century Mediterranean world, some ailments forced individuals to live outside of the community. In other words, they were considered impure and were not able to participate fully in the group. While the sickness might not immediately lead to "physical" death, they were certainly deadly in their own way. A powerful example of this was leprosy. Those with this skin condition experienced alienation. They experienced a very real social death. It is in this situation that Jesus also brought unexpected new life. The author of Matthew recounts a story of an encounter between Jesus and a leper (8:1–4). Jesus, coming down from a mountain, is followed by a great crowd. In the crowd, is a leper. The leper kneels down before Jesus and says, "Lord, if you choose, you can make me clean." Jesus stretches out his hand and touches the leper. Along with the touch, he announces, "I do choose. Be made clean!" At once the leprosy is cleansed. In this story, and in many other similar narratives, Jesus both "cures" and "heals." The leprosy is cleansed. In other words, Jesus is described as performing the physical act of curing the leper. However, Jesus also performs the (perhaps more important) social act of healing. Through the cleansing of the leper, the individual is once again free to be an active member of the community. In other words, the rift between the leper and the community has been healed. While the curing of the ailment does highlight the theme of unexpected new life, the theme is also powerfully present in the social act of healing. For the leper, living outside of the community is a form of social death. It is in the midst of this death that Jesus brings unexpected new life. The leper, therefore, experiences the reality of new life in two ways: through the curing of the leprosy and the healing of the community alienation.

It is not only in the deeds of Jesus that new life emerges from expected death, this theme is also present in his teaching. In 10:34–39, Jesus proclaims that he comes not to bring peace, but a sword:

> Do not think that I have come to bring peace to the earth; I have not come to bring peace, but a sword. For I have come to set a man against his father, and a daughter against her mother, and a daughter-in-law against her mother-in-law; and one's foes will be members of one's own household. Whoever loves father or mother more than me is not worthy of me; and whoever loves son or daughter more than me is not worthy of me; and whosever does not take up the cross and follow me is not worthy of me. Those who find their live will lose it, and those who lose their life for my sake will find it.

While the various interpretations of this verse are hotly debated and the verse itself may seem controversial, the author once again weaves in the theme of unexpected new life. The family was the primary social group in ancient Palestine. This means that family members were fiercely loyal to one another. The family was the center of all of daily life. Quite simply, one could not survive outside of the family group. In this short teaching, Jesus challenges this social norm. There is little doubt that the actions of the earliest Christ-followers were regarded with hostility from their families, for Jesus emphasized that following him takes precedence over the family. In the first-century Mediterranean world, this proclamation would have sounded like "social death." And yet, Jesus proclaims, "those who lose their life for my sake will find it." In this teaching, Jesus makes note that when followers commit to him, rather than experiencing the expected (social/familial) death, they will experience a surprising, unexpected new life in him.

The theme that from expected death comes unexpected new life is also emphasized in many of Jesus' parables. For example, in 18:10–14, Jesus asks a crowd, "What do you think? If a shepherd has a hundred sheep, and one of them has gone astray, does he not leave the ninety-nine on the mountain and go in search of the one that went astray?" Jesus continues by describing the joy that is felt when the one lost sheep is finally found. The shepherd rejoices over it more than over the ninety-nine that never went astray. While this parable may be interpreted in various ways, it does again reveal the author's theme of new life. It is a great risk to leave ninety-nine sheep to search for one. But in this parable, there is great rejoicing when the expected loss, the expected death, of one sheep turns into the unexpected discovery, the unexpected new life, of the animal.

Finally, the theme of expected death and unexpected new life is not only woven into the story of the life, actions, and teaching of Jesus, but it is also the foundation for the commissioning of the twelve disciples (10:5–15). Jesus instructs his followers to "proclaim the good news, 'the kingdom of heaven has come near.' Cure the sick, raise the dead, cleanse the lepers, cast out demons." In other words, just as Jesus has offered new life to the sick in both curing and healing, the disciples are to bring unexpected new life to those expecting and experiencing death. Just as Jesus raised a girl from the dead, the disciples are to bring new life to those in the midst of mourning. This mission is made all the more powerful when we recall that the disciples themselves also experienced this radical reversal of fortunes. While experiencing a storm at sea, they were given unexpected new life. While trading loyalty to their families for loyalty to Jesus, they were given unexpected new life in him. It is now their mission also to be agents of unexpected new life.

The Death and Resurrection of Jesus

FROM EXPECTED DEATH COMES UNEXPECTED NEW LIFE

It is beyond dispute that the culmination of Matthew's gospel is the death and resurrection of Jesus. While the birth of Jesus is told in eight verses, the story of his death and resurrection spreads over three chapters (26–28). After following the theme of expected death and unexpected new life throughout the gospel, the most powerful example of this reversal of fortunes occurs here. The crucifixion of Jesus is a violent murder. This is much more than expected death. Jesus is truly killed. Three days later, the most unexpected of events occurs. In the resurrection, Jesus experiences new life. The theme that the author introduces with the image of the womb and of birth finally culminates with the tomb and new life.

It is difficult to say where the story of Jesus' death and resurrection actually begins. According to the author, Jesus foretells the event four times during his public ministry (16:21–23; 17:22–23; 20:17–19; and 26:1–2). Furthermore, many important events lead up to his crucifixion. For example, Jesus celebrates the Passover with the disciples (26:17–30), he foretells

Peter's denial (26:31–35), Jesus prays at Gethsemane (26:36–46), and Jesus is betrayed by Judas and arrested (26:47–56). After his arrest, Jesus is brought before the high priest, Caiaphas, (26:57–68) and before the governor, Pilate (27:1–2, 11–26). Regardless of where the story starts, it is clear where the story is expected to end.

Jesus is flogged and mocked and made to wear a crown of thorns. Soldiers place a reed in his right hand and kneel before him. They hiss, "Hail, King of the [Judeans]." He is finally led away to be crucified at a place called Golgotha (which means Place of a Skull). From noon on, darkness comes over the whole land until three in the afternoon. The darkness indicates that even nature grieves. Even nature *expects* the death of Jesus. Jesus himself cries out, "My God, my God, why have you forsaken me?" At that moment the curtain in the temple is torn in two, from top to bottom. The earth shakes and the rocks are split. Nowhere in Matthew's gospel is death more vividly described. In the evening, a rich man from Arimathea, named Joseph asks Pilate if he may take the body of Jesus that he may receive a proper burial. The body is wrapped in clean linen cloth and is laid in a new tomb which has been hewn in rock. Joseph of Arimathea then rolls a great stone to the door of the tomb and walks away.

At this point in the story, the theme that from expected death comes unexpected new life is made powerfully clear. Not even death on a cross is able to stop God's plan for new life. After the Sabbath, as the first day of the week is dawning, Mary Magdalene and the other Mary go to see the tomb. Suddenly there is a great earthquake. Just as nature itself mourned the death of Jesus with darkness and the shaking of the earth, nature here seems to quake with joy. An angel of the Lord descends from heaven and rolls back the stone. The angel says to the women, "Do not be afraid; I know that you are looking for Jesus who was crucified. He is not here; for he has been raised, as he said. Come, see the place where he lay. Then go quickly and tell his disciples, 'He has been raised from the dead, and indeed he is going ahead of you to Galilee; there you will see him.' This is my message for you" (28:5–7).

The birth of Jesus and his death and resurrection make perfect "book-ends" for the theme of new life. It is expected that Jesus will be killed while still in the womb. As Joseph agonizes over his dilemma, he is visited by an angel of the Lord. From this situation of expected death comes unexpected new life. The theme weaves throughout the ministry of Jesus. Both literally and metaphorically, new life emerges from death in the deeds and words of Jesus. Again at the end of the story, unexpected new life triumphs over death, even death on a cross.

Conclusion

This book offers a "micro-thesis" and a "macro-thesis." The smaller thesis is that the context of the birth narrative in Matthew's gospel is that of an honor killing. Mary is pregnant and it is assumed that she has committed adultery. In first-century Palestine, the act of adultery brought shame upon the family. Killing the adulteress was thought to restore family honor. Joseph's dilemma, then, is between exposure and secrecy. If Joseph exposes Mary's pregnancy, he is handing her over to death. If Joseph keeps Mary's pregnancy a secret, he is going against the law of the Lord. What is a righteous man to do?

The larger thesis is that the birth narrative in Matthew introduces a theme that weaves throughout the gospel, *from expected death comes unexpected new life*. From the womb to the tomb, the death of Jesus is expected. However, where there is expected death, Jesus experiences unexpected new life. But the story does not stop here. Jesus is also depicted as the agent of new life. Jesus offers new life to those who are expecting death. Whether the death is literal or metaphorical, physical or social, Jesus brings new life. And yet, this is still not the end of the story. The author of Matthew describes the mission of Jesus's disciples. They, too, are to be agents of new life. The disciples are to live in the midst of death, all of the while bringing the unexpected. And still, there is more. The author of Matthew's gospel compels the audience to be agents of life. Generations of listeners and readers are commissioned to offer the unexpected to those experiencing sickness, brokenness, alienation, and death. It is remarkable that this important theme, this good news, all begins with an expected honor killing.

Bibliography

Abu-Hilal, Ahmad. "Arab and North-American Social Attitudes: Some Cross-Cultural Comparisons." *Mankind Quarterly* 22 (1982) 193–207.

Abu-Lughod, Leila. *Veiled Sentiments: Honor and Piety in a Bedouin Society*. Berkeley: University of California Press, 1986.

Abu-Odeh, Lama. "Crimes of Honour and the Construction of Gender in Arab Society." In *Feminism and Islam: Legal and Literary Perspectives*, edited by Mai Yamani, 141–94. New York: New York University Press, 1996.

Abu-Toameh, Khaled. "Report says Palestinian 'Honor Killings' are Increasing." *The Jerusalem Post*, May 30, 2007, p. 3.

Afkhami, Mahnaz. *Faith & Freedom: Women's Human Rights in the Muslim World*. Syracuse: Syracuse University Press, 1995.

Agence France Presse. "One in 10 British Asians backs honour killings: poll." September 4, 2006.

Ahmed, Leila. *Women and Gender in Islam: Historical Roots of a Modern Debate*. New Haven, CT: Yale University Press, 1992.

Albright, W. F. and C. S. Mann. *Matthew*. The Anchor Bible 26. New York: Doubleday, 1971.

al-Fanar (Palestinian Feminist Organization). "Developments in the Struggle against the Murder of Women against the Background of So-called Family Honor." *Women Against Fundamentalism Journal* 6 (1995) 37–41.

al-Khayyat, Sana. *Honour and Shame: Women in Modern Iraq*. London: Saqi Books, 1990.

Allison, Dale C. "Divorce, Celibacy and Joseph (Matthew 1.18–25 and 19.1–12)." *Journal for the Study of the New Testament* 49 (1993) 3–10.

al-Malaika, Nazik. *A Tranquil Moment of a Wave*. Beirut, 1957.

Altizer, Thomas J. J. *The Contemporary Jesus*. Albany, NY: State University of New York Press, 1997.

Anderson, Janice Capel. "Mary's Difference: Gender and Patriarchy in the Birth Narratives." *Journal of Religion* 67 (1987) 183–202.

Antonelli, Alessandra. "Crimes Not Stories." *Palestine Report* (1998) 13, 16.

Antoun, Richard T. *Arab Village: A Social Structural Study of a Trans-Jordanian Peasant Community*. Bloomington, IN: Indiana University Press, 1972.

73

Araji, S. K. and J. Carlson. "Family Violence Including Crimes of Honor in Jordan." *Violence Against Women* 7 (2001) 586–621.

Argyle, A. W. *The Gospel According to Matthew.* Cambridge: Cambridge University Press, 1963.

Baker, N. V., P. R. Gregware, and M. A. Cassidy. "Family Killing Fields: Honor rationales in the Murder of Women." *Violence Against Women* 5 (1999) 164–84.

Barton, Carlin A. *Roman Honor: The Fire in the Bones.* Berkeley: University of California Press, 2001.

Beare, Francis Wright. *The Gospel According to Matthew: A Commentary.* Oxford: Basil Blackwell, 1981.

Benson, G. P. "Virgin Birth, Virgin Conception." *The Expository Times* 98 (1987) 139–40.

Beyer, Lisa, and Jo LeGood. "The Price of Honor: Jordanians are Fighting a Brutal Arab Tradition—The Murder of Women for Alleged Sexual Impropriety." *Time* 153 (1999) 55.

Bilefsky, Dan. "How to Avoid Honor Killing in Turkey? Honor Suicide." *The New York Times,* July 16, 2006, sec. 1.

Bird, Steve. "'My Family Said I Had Destroyed Their Name.'" *The Times (London),* June 13, 2007, p. 15.

———. "'Honour' Killing Used to Threaten Others." *The Times (London),* June 13, 2007, p. 15.

Blomberg, Craig, L. "The Liberation of Illegitimacy: Women and Rulers in Matthew 1–2." *Biblical Theology Bulletin* 21 (1991) 145–50.

Boling, Robert G. *Judges.* The Anchor Bible 6A. Garden City: Doubleday, 1975.

Boring, M. Eugene. *Matthew.* The New Interpreter's Bible 8. Nashville: Abingdon Press, 1995.

Bornkamm, Günther, Gerhard Barth, and Heinz Joachim Held. *Tradition and Interpretation in Matthew.* Translated by Percy Scott. Philadelphia: Westminster, 1963.

Boslooper, Thomas. "Jesus' Virgin Birth and Non-Christian 'Parallels.'" *Religion in Life* 26 (1956–57) 87–97.

———. *The Virgin Birth.* Philadelphia: Westminster, 1962.

Bostock, Gerald. "Virgin Birth or Human Conception?" *The Expository Times* 97 (1986) 260–63.

Bourdieu, Pierre. "The Sentiment of Honour in Kabyle Society." In *Honour and Shame,* edited by J. G. Peristiany, 191–241. London: Weidenfeld and Nicholson, 1966.

Bourke, Myles M. Review of *The Birth of the Messiah: A Commentary on the Infancy Narratives in Matthew and Luke,* by Raymond E. Brown. *The Catholic Biblical Quarterly* 40 (1978) 120–24.

Bowen, Donna Lee and Evelyn A. Early. *Everyday Life in the Muslim Middle East.* 2nd ed. Bloomington, IN: Indiana University Press, 2002.

Brandes, Stanley. "Reflections on Honor and Shame in the Mediterranean." In *Honor and Shame in the Unity of the Mediterranean,* edited by David D. Gilmore, 121–34. Washington DC: American Anthropological Association, 1987.

Brayford, Susan A. "To Shame or Not to Shame: Sexuality in the Mediterranean Diaspora." *Semeia* 87 (1999) 163–76.

Brooks, Geraldine. *Nine Parts of Desire: The Hidden World of Islamic Women.* New York: Anchor, 1995.

Brown, Raymond E. "The Problem of the Virginal Conception of Jesus." *Theological Studies* 33/1 (March 1972) 3–34.

———. *The Virginal Conception and Bodily Resurrection of Jesus*. New York: Paulist, 1973.

———. "Gospel Infancy Narrative Research from 1976 to 1986: Part 1 (Matthew)." *Catholic Biblical Quarterly* 48/3 (July 1986) 468–83.

———. *The Birth of the Messiah: A Commentary on the Infancy Narratives in Matthew and Luke*. New York: Doubleday, 1993.

Buchanan, George Wesley. *The Gospel of Matthew*. The Mellen Biblical Commentary 1. Eugene, OR: Wipf and Stock, 2006. First published 1996 by Mellen Biblical. Page references are to 1996 edition.

Burn, Shawn Meghan. *Women Across Cultures: A Global Perspective*. 2nd ed. New York: McGraw-Hill, 2005.

Calkins, Arthur Burton. "The Justice of Joseph Revisited." In *Kecharitōmenē*, 165–77. Paris: Desclée, 1990.

Campbell, J. K. *Honour, Family, and Patronage: A Study of Institutions and Moral Values in a Greek Mountain Community*. New York: Oxford University Press, 1974.

Caner, Ergun Mehmet. *Voices Behind the Veil: The World of Islam Through the Eyes of Women*. Grand Rapids, MI: Kregel, 2004.

Carnell, Edward John. "The Virgin Birth of Christ." *Christianity Today* (December 7, 1959) 9–10.

Carr, A. *The Gospel According to St Matthew: With Maps, Notes, and Introduction*. Cambridge: Cambridge University Press, 1890.

Carter, Warren. *Matthew and the Margins: A Sociopolitical and Religious Reading*. Maryknoll, NY: Orbis, 2000.

———. *Matthew: Storyteller, Interpreter, Evangelist*. Peabody, MA: Hendrickson, 1996.

Cave, C. H. "St. Matthew's Infancy Narrative." *New Testament Studies* 9 (1962–63) 382–90.

Chance, John K. "The Anthropology of Honor and Shame: Culture, Values, and Practice." *Semeia* 68 (1996) 139–51.

Charlesworth, James H. editor. *The Old Testament Pseudepigrapha*. Vol. 2. New York: Doubleday, 1985.

Chrysostom, John. *The Homilies of St. John Chrysostom, Archbishop of Constantinople, On the Gospel of St. Matthew*. Translated by Sir George Prevost. Revised, with notes, by M. B. Riddle. New York: Christian Literature, 1886.

Clark, Alan C. "The Virgin Birth: A Theological Reappraisal." *Theological Studies* 34 (1973) 576–93.

Combs-Schilling, M. E. *Sacred Performances: Islam, Sexuality and Sacrifice*. New York: Columbia University Press, 1989.

Coulson, Noel J. "Regulation of Sexual Behavior under Traditional Islamic Law." In *Society and the Sexes in Medieval Islam*, edited by Afaf Lutfi Al-Sayyid Marsot, 63–68. Malibu: Undena, 1977.

Cox, G. E. P. *The Gospel According to Saint Matthew: Introduction and Commentary*. London: SCM, 1958.

Cranfield, C. E. B. "Some Reflections on the Subject of the Virgin Birth." *Scottish Journal of Theology* 41/2 (1988) 177–89.

Crouch, James E. "How Early Christians Viewed the Birth of Jesus." *Bible Review* 7 (1991) 34–38.

Daniélou, Jean. *The Infancy Narratives*. New York: Herder & Herder. 1968.

Davies, Margaret. *Matthew*. Sheffield: JSOT Press, 1993.

Davis, J. *People of the Mediterranean: An Essay in Comparative Social Anthropology*. London: Routledge & Kegan Paul, 1977.

Delaney, Carol. "Seeds of Honor, Fields of Shame." In *Honor and Shame in the Unity of the Mediterranean*, edited by David D. Gilmore, 35–48. Washington, DC: American Anthropological Association, 1987.

deSilva, David A. *Despising Shame: Honor Discourse and Community Maintenance in the Epistle to the Hebrews*. Atlanta: Scholars, 1995.

Didur, Jill and Teresa Heffernan. "Revisiting the Subaltern in the New Empire." *Cultural Studies*, 17 (2003) 1–15.

Dodd, Peter C. "Family Honor and the Forces of Change in Arab Society." *International Journal of Middle East Studies* 4 (1973) 40–54.

Dodds, Paisley. "Father Guilty in 'Honor Killing.'" *Chicago Tribune*, June 12, 2007, sec. 1, p. 12.

Doumanis, Mariella. *Mothering in Greece: From Collectivism to Individualism*. London: Academic, 1983.

Down, M. J. "The Matthean Birth Narratives: Matthew 1:18–2:23." *Expository Times* 90 (1978–79) 51–52.

Dunne, Bruce. "Power and Sexuality in the Middle East." *Middle East Report* 28 (1998) 8–11.

Duzkan, A. and F. Kocali. "An Honor Killing: She Fled, Her Throat Was Cut." In *Women and Sexuality in Muslim Societies*, edited by Pinar Ilkkaracan, 381–87. Istanbul: Women for Women's Human Rights, 2000.

Edwards, Douglas. *The Virgin Birth in History and Faith*. London: Faber & Faber, 1943.

Edwards, Richard A. *Matthew's Story of Jesus*. Philadelphia: Fortress, 1985.

Ehrman, Bart D. *After the New Testament: A Reader in Early Christianity*. New York: Oxford University Press, 1999.

Elass, Rasha. "'Honor' Killing Spurs Outcry in Syria." *Christian Science Monitor*, February 24, 2007, p. 7.

Elliott, J. K. *The Apocryphal Jesus: Legends of the Early Church*. Oxford: Oxford University Press, 1996.

———. *A Synopsis of the Apocryphal Nativity and Infancy Narratives*. Leiden: Brill, 2006.

———, editor. *The Apocryphal New Testament: A Collection of Apocryphal Christian Literature in an English Translation based on M. R. James*. New York: Oxford, 2005.

El Saadawi, Nawal. *The Hidden Face of Eve: Women in the Arab World*. Translated and edited by Sherif Hetata. Boston: Beacon, 1982.

Emery, James. "Reputation is Everything: Honor Killings Among the Palestinians." *The World and I* (May 2003) 182–91.

Erdman, Charles, R. *The Gospel of Matthew*. Philadelphia: Westminster, 1948.

Esler, Philip F. *The First Christians in the Social Worlds: Social-Scientific Approaches to New Testament Interpretation*. London: Routledge, 1994.

Evans, Martin. "Killed by her Own Family for 'Honour.'" *The Express*, July 15, 2006, p. 16.

Fenton, J. C. *Saint Matthew*. Westminster Pelican Commentaries. Philadelphia: Westminster, 1963.

Filson, Floyd V. *A Commentary on the Gospel According to St. Matthew*. London: Adam & Charles Black, 1960.

Finkelstein, J. J. "Sex Offenses in Sumerian Laws." *Journal of the American Oriental Society* 86 (1966) 362–63.

Fitzmyer, Joseph A. "The Virginal Conception of Jesus in the New Testament." *Theological Studies* 34 (1973) 541–75.

France, R. T. "Scripture, Tradition and History in the Infancy Narratives of Matthew." In *Gospel Perspectives*, vol. 2, *Studies of History and Tradition in the Four Gospels*, edited by R. T. France and David Wenham, 239–66. Sheffield: JSOT Press, 1981.

———. *The Gospel According to Matthew: An Introduction and Commentary*. New International Commentary on the New Testament. Grand Rapids, MI: Eerdmans, 1985.

Franchetti, Mark. "Iraqi Women Die in 'Honour' Murders." *The Sunday Times (London)*, September 28, 2003, p. 25.

Freed, Edwin D. "The Women in Matthew's Genealogy." *Journal for the Study of the New Testament* 29 (1987) 3–19.

———. *The Stories of Jesus' Birth: A Critical Introduction*. Sheffield: Sheffield Academic, 2001.

Gairola, Rahul. "Burning with Shame: Desire and South Asian Patriarchy, from Gayatri Spivak's 'Can the Subaltern Speak?' to Deepa Mehta's *Fire*." *Comparative Literature* 54 (2002) 307–24.

Garland, David E. *Reading Matthew: A Literary and Theological Commentary on the First Gospel*. London: SPCK, 1993.

Gilmore, David D., editor. *Honor and Shame and the Unity of the Mediterranean*. Washington DC: American Anthropological Association, 1987.

Gilmore, David D. "Introduction: The Shame of Dishonor." In *Honor and Shame in the Unity of the Mediterranean*, edited by David D. Gilmore, 2–21. Washington DC: American Anthropological Association, 1987.

Goldstein, Matthew A. "The Biological Roots of Heat-of-Passion Crimes and Honor Killings." *Politics and the Life Sciences* 21 (2002) 28–37.

Goodenough, Patrick. "Blood and Honor." *Middle East Digest* (February 1995) 1–5.

Goodwin, Jan. *Price of Honour: Muslim Women Lift the Veil of Silence on the Islamic World*. London: Warner, 1995.

Green, F. W. *The Gospel According to Saint Matthew*. Oxford: Clarendon, 1936.

Green, H. Benedict. *The Gospel According to Matthew*. Oxford: Oxford University Press, 1975.

Gregg, Gary S. *The Middle East: A Cultural Psychology*. Oxford: Oxford University Press, 2005.

Gundy, Robert H. *Matthew: A Commentary on His Literary and Theological Art*. Grand Rapids, MI: Eerdmans, 1982.

———. *Matthew: A Commentary on His Handbook for a Mixed Church under Persecution*. Grand Rapids, MI: Eerdmans, 1994.

Haeri, S. "The Politics of Dishonor: Rape and Power in Pakistan." In *Faith and Freedom: Women's Human Rights in the Muslim World*, edited by M. Afkhami. 167–74. Syracuse: Syracuse University Press, 1995.

Hagner, Donald A. *Matthew 1–13*. Word Biblical Commentary 33A. CD-ROM. Nelson Reference & Electronic, 1993.

Hamzeh-Muhaisen, Muna. "Violence Against Women: Who Will Stop the Men?" *Palestine Report* (October 10, 1997) 4–5.

Hanson, K. C., and Douglas E. Oakman. *Palestine in the Time of Jesus: Social Structures and Social Conflicts*. Minneapolis: Fortress, 2002.

Hare, Douglas R. A. *Matthew*. Interpretation: A Bible Commentary for Teaching and Preaching. Louisville: John Knox, 1993.

Harrington, Daniel J. *The Gospel of Matthew*. Sacra Pagina 1. Collegeville, MD: Liturgical, 1991.

Hasan, Manar. "The Politics of Honor: Patriarchy, the State and the Murder of Women in the Name of Family Honor." *The Journal of Israeli History* 21 (2002) 1–37.

Hawley, Richard, and Barbara Levick, editors. *Women in Antiquity: New Assessments*. London: Routledge, 1995.

Hegland, Mary Elaine. "Gender and Islam: Women's Accommodating Resistance" In *Social History of Women and Gender in the Modern Middle East*, edited by Margaret L. Meriwether and Judith E. Tucker, 186–97. Boulder, CO: Westview, 1999.

Hendrickx, Herman. *The Infancy Narratives*. London: Geoffrey Chapman, 1984.

Hill, David. *The Gospel of Matthew*. London: Oliphants, 1978.

Hinkle, Steve, and Rupert Brown. "Intergroup Comparison and Social Identity: Some Links and Lacunae." In *Social Identity Theory: Constructive and Critical Advances*, edited by Dominic Abrams and Michael A. Hogg, 48–70. New York: Harvester-Wheatsheaf, 1990.

Hock, Ronald F. *The Infancy Gospels of James and Thomas: With Introductions, Notes, and Original Text Featuring the New Scholars Version Translation*. Scholars Bible. Santa Rosa, CA: Polebridge, 1995.

———. *The Life of Mary and Birth of Jesus*. Berkeley: Ulysses, 1997

Horden, Peregrine and Nicholas Purcell. *The Corrupting Sea: A Study of Mediterranean History*. Oxford: Blackwell, 2000.

Horsley, Richard A. *The Liberation of Christmas: The Infancy Narratives in Social Context*. New York: Continuum, 1989.

Ilkkaracan, Pinar. "Exploring the Context of Women's Sexuality in Eastern Turkey." *Reproductive Health Matters* 6 (1998) 66–75.

Instone-Brewer, David. *Divorce and Remarriage in the Bible: The Social and Literary Context*. Grand Rapids, MI: Eerdmans, 2002.

Jaber, Hala. "'Honour' Killings Grow as Girl, 17, Stoned to Death." *The Times (London)*, November 4, 2007, p. 25.

Jehl, Douglas. "For Shame: A Special Report. Arab Honor's Price: A Woman's Blood." *The New York Times*, June 20, 1999, sec. 1, p. 1.

Jones, Ivor H. *The Gospel of Matthew*. London: Epworth, 1994.

Josephus. Translated by H. St. J. Thackery et al. 10 vols. Loeb Classical Library. Cambridge: Harvard University Press, 1926–1965.

Judd, Terri. "Stabbed to Death as Her Family Watched . . . for Honour." *The Independent (London)*, July 15, 2006, p. 18.

Juschka, Amy. "The Binary Hoax: Honour Killings in the Middle east or a Massacre in Montreal—Recognizing Expressions of Patriarchy." *Briarpatch* 34 (2005) 21–23.

Keddie, Nikki R. *Women in the Middle East: Past and Present*. Princeton, NJ: Princeton University Press, 2007.

Keener, Craig S. *A Commentary on the Gospel of Matthew*. Grand Rapids, MI: Eerdmans, 1999.

Kent, Paul. "Young Love . . . Two Ancient Religions . . . A Women Dying in a Pool of her Own Blood After a Public Stoning: The Price Dua'a Paid." *Hobart Mercury (Australia)*, May 24, 2007, p. 9.

Khaki, M. Aslam. *Honour, Killings in Pakistan & Islamic View*. Islamabad: Insaaf Welfare Trust, 2004.

Khan, Sheema. "Uprooting Age-Old Customs from Within: Muslims Must Speak Out Against Such Practices as Honor Killings and Female Genital Mutilation." *The Globe and Mail (Canada)*, October 9, 2007, sec. A, p. 21.

Khanum, Saeeda, director. *Love, Honor, & Disobey*. Faction Films, 2005.

Kim, Elizabeth. *Ten Thousand Sorrows*. New York: Doubleday, 2000.

Kingsbury, Jack Dean. *Matthew: Structure, Christology, Kingdom*. Philadelphia: Fortress, 1975.

Korvarik, Chiara Angela. *Interviews with Muslim Women of Pakistan*. Minneapolis: Syren, 2004.

Kosmoszewski, J. Ed, M. James Sawyer, and Daniel B. Wallace. *Reinventing Jesus: How Contemporary Skeptics Miss the Real Jesus and Mislead Popular Culture*. Grand Rapids, MI: Kregel, 2006.

Kress, Rory. "Gazans Suspect Murder of Sisters was Honor Killing." *The Jerusalem Post*, July 25, 2007, p. 6.

Kulwicki, A. D. "The Practice of Honor Crimes: A Glimpse of Domestic Violence in the Arab World." *Issues In Mental Health Nursing* 23 (2002) 77–87.

Laurentin, René. *The Truth of Christmas: Beyond the Myths*. Translated by Micahel J. Wrenn. Petersham: St. Bede's. 1986.

Lawrence, Louise Joy. *An Ethnography of the Gospel of Matthew: A Critical Assessment of the Use of the Honour and Shame Model in New Testament Studies*. Tübingen: Mohr Siebeck, 2003.

Leaney, A. R. C. "Birth Narratives in St Luke and St Matthew." *New Testament Studies* 8 (1962) 158–66.

Lefkowitz, Mary R., and Maureen B. Fant. *Women's Life in Greece and Rome: A Source Book in Translation*. 3rd ed. Baltimore: The Johns Hopkins University Press, 2005.

Levine, Amy-Jill, and Marianne Blickenstaff, editors. *A Feminist Companion to Matthew*. Sheffield: Sheffield Academic, 2001.

Levinson, Bernard M. *Deuteronomy and the Hermeneutics of Legal Innovation*. Oxford: Oxford University Press, 2002.

Livy. Translated by B. O. Foster et al. 14 vols. Loeb Classical Library. Cambridge: Harvard University Press, 1919–1959.

Logmans, A., A. Verhoeff, R. Bol Raap, R. Creighton, and M. van Lent. "Ethical Dilemma: Should Doctors Reconstruct the Vaginal Introitus of Adolescent Girls to Mimic the Virginal State? (Who Wants the Procedure and Why)." *British Medical Journal* 316 (1998) 459–60.

Loudon, Bruce. "Pakistan Police Fail as 'Honour' Killings Soar." *Weekend Australian*. February 10, 2007, p. 16.

————. "Pakistan's 'Honour Killers' Go Free." *Weekend Australian*. February 10, 2007, p. 16.

Lüdemann, Gerd. *Virgin Birth? The Real Story of Mary and Her Son Jesus*. Translated by John Bowden. London: SCM, 1998.

Lurie, Danielle, director. *In the Morning*. Produced by Katie Mustard. Women Make Movies, 2004.

Luz, Ulrich. *Matthew 1–7: A Commentary*. Translated by Wilhelm C. Linss. Edinburgh: T. & T. Clark, 1990.

Machen, J. Gresham. *The Virgin Birth of Christ*. New York: Harper & Brothers, 1930.

Malina, Bruce J. *Windows on the World of Jesus: Time Travel to Ancient Judea*. Louisville: Westminster John Knox, 1993.

————. *The New Testament World: Insights from Cultural Anthropology*. 3rd ed. Louisville: Westminster John Knox, 2001.

Malina, Bruce J., and Richard L. Rohrbaugh. *Social-Science Commentary on the Synoptic Gospels*. Minneapolis: Fortress, 1992.

————. *Social-Science Commentary on the Gospel of John*. Minneapolis: Fortress, 1998.

Marohl, Matthew J. *Faithfulness and the Purpose of Hebrews: A Social Identity Approach*. Princeton Theological Monograph Series 82. Eugene, OR: Pickwick, 2008.

Massaux, E. *The Influence of the Gospel of Matthew on Christian Literature before Saint Irenaeus*. 2 vols. Translated by N. Belval and S. Hecht. New Gospel Studies 5. Atlanta: Mercer University Press, 1990.

Matthews, Victor H. "Honor and Shame in Gender-Related Legal Situations in the Hebrew Bible." In *Gender and Law in the Hebrew Bible and the Ancient Near East*, edited by Victor H. Matthews, Bernard M. Levinson, and Tikva Frymer-Kensky, 97–112. Journal for the Study of the Old Testament Supplement 262. Sheffield: Sheffield Academic, 1998.

McCann, J. Clinton. *Judges*. Interpretation: A Bible Commentary for Teaching and Preaching. Louisville: John Knox, 2002.

McGreal, Chris. "Murdered in the Name of Family Honour: Chris McGreal Reports from Ramallah on a Rise in Killings of Palestinian Women." *The Guardian (London)*, July 1, 2005, p. 18.

McKeating, Henry. "Sanctions Against Adultery in Ancient Israelite Society, with Some Reflections on Methodology in the Study of Old Testament Ethics." *Journal for the Study of the Old Testament* 11 (1979) 57–63.

Mernissi, Fatima. "Virginity and Patriarchy." *Women's Studies International Forum* 5 (1982) 183–91.

Metzger, Bruce M. *An Introduction to The Apocrypha*. New York: Oxford University Press, 1969.

Micklem, Philip A. *St Matthew*. London: Methuen, 1917.

Migne, Jacques Paul, editor. *Patrologiae Cursus Completus*. Series Graeca. 166 volumes. Paris: Migne, 1857–1866.

Miller, Karyn and Tom Harper. "'Honour Killings' Increasing in Britain as Women Stand Up for their Rights." *The Sunday Telegraph (London)*, July 16, 2006, p. 10.

Minear, Paul S. *Matthew: The Teacher's Gospel*. London: Darton, Longman, and Todd, 1982.

The Mishnah. Translated by Herbert Danby. Oxford: Oxford University Press, 1933.

The Mishnah: A New Translation. Translated by Jacob Neusner. New Haven: Yale University Press, 1988.

M'Neile, Alan Hugh. *The Gospel According to St. Matthew*. London: MacMillan, 1915.

Moghaizel, Laure. "The Arab and Mediterranean World: Legislation Toward Crimes of Honor." In *Empowerment and the Law: Strategies of Third World Women*, edited by Margaret Schuler, 174–80. Washington, DC: OEF International, 1986.

Mojab, Shahrzad. "'Honor Killing': Culture, Politics, and Theory." *Middle East Women's Studies Review* 17 (2002) 1–7.

Mojab, Shahrzad, and Amir Hassanpour. "Thoughts on the Struggle against 'Honor Killing.'" *The International Journal of Kurdish Studies* 16 (2002) 83–97.

———. "The Politics and Culture of 'Honor Killing': The Murder of Fadime Şahindal." *Pakistan Journal of Women's Studies: Alam-e-Niswan* 9 (2002) 57–77.

Morris, Leon. *The Gospel According to Matthew*. Grand Rapids, MI: Eerdmans, 1992.

Mosquera, Patricia M. Rodriguez, et al. "Honor in the Mediterranean and Northern Europe." *Journal of Cross-Cultural Psychology* 33 (2002) 16–36.

Mounce, Robert H. *Matthew*. New International Biblical Commentary. Peabody, MA: Hendrickson, 1991.

Moxnes, Halvor. "Honor and Shame." In *The Social Sciences and New Testament Interpretation*, edited by Richard Rohrbaugh, 19–40. Peabody, MA: Hendrickson, 1996.

———. *Putting Jesus in His Place: A Radical Vision of Household and Kingdom*. Louisville: Westminster John Knox, 2003.

Mulholland, M. Robert Jr. "The Infancy Narratives in Matthew and Luke: Of History, Theology, and Literature." *Biblical Archaeology Review* 7 (March/April 1981) 46–59.

Naber, Nadine. "Teaching about Honor Killings and Other Sensitive Topics in Middle East Studies." *Middle East Women's Study Review* 15 (2002) 20–21.

Narayan, Uma. "Cross-Cultural Connections, Border-Crossings, and 'Death by Culture:' Thinking about Dowry-Murders in India and Domestic-Violence Murders in the United States." In *Dislocating Cultures: Identities, Traditions, and Third World Feminism*, 81–117. New York: Routledge, 1997.

Naylor, Larry L. *American Culture: Myth and Reality of a Culture of Diversity*. Westport: Bergin & Garvey, 1998.

Neighbour, Margaret. "Honour Killing Plea to Pakistan's Leader." *The Scotsman*, September 21, 2005, p. 25.

Newell, Katherine S., Elin Ross, Carrie McVicker, and Jen Cromwell. *Discrimination Against the Girl Child: Female Infanticide, Female Genital Cutting, and Honor Killing*. Series on International Youth Issues 6. Washington DC: Youth Advocate Program International, 2000.

Neyrey, Jerome H. *Honor and Shame in the Gospel of Matthew*. Louisville: Westminster John Knox, 1998.

Nickerson, Colin. "For Muslim Women, A Deadly Defiance: 'Honor Killings' on Rise in Europe." *The Boston Globe*, January 16, 2006, sec. A, p. 1.

Nolland, John. "The Four (Five) Women and Other Annotations in Matthew's Genealogy." *New Testament Studies* 43 (1997) 527–39.

Nowell, Irene. "Jesus' Great-Grandmothers: Matthew's Four and More." *Catholic Biblical Quarterly* 70 (2008) 1–15.

Olson, Dennis T. "The Book of Judges." In *The New Interpreter's Bible* 2:721–888. Nashville: Abingdon, 1998.

Osiek, Carolyn, Margaret Y. Macdonald, with Janet H. Tulloch. *A Woman's Place: House Churches in Earliest Christianity*. Minneapolis: Fortress, 2006.

Our Honour, His Glory. Norsk Rikskringkasting, producer. Sveriges Television. New York: Filmakers Library, 1997.

Palestinian Human Rights Monitoring Group. "Honor Killing: Killing Women on the Basis of Family Honor." *The Monitor* 6, August 2002. http://www.phrmg.org/monitor.2002/Aug2002.htm.

Palestinian Ma'an News Agency. "Palesinian Agency says 2006 'Bloodiest Year' for 'Honour Killings.'" English translation by the BBC Monitoring Middle East. December 4, 2006.

Parrot, Andrea and Nina Cummings. *Forsaken Females: The Global Brutalization of Women*. Lanham: Rowan & Littlefield, 2006.

Patte, Daniel. *The Gospel According to Matthew: A Structural Commentary on Matthew's Faith*. Philadelphia: Fortress, 1987.

Peake, Arthur S. "The Supernatural Birth of Jesus." *The Methodist Quarterly Review* 73 (1924) 579–91.

Pelikan, Jaroslav. *Jesus Throughout the Centuries: His Place in the History of Culture*. New Haven, CT: Yale University Press, 1985.

Peristiany, J. G., editor. *Honour and Grace in Anthropology*. Cambridge: Cambridge University Press, 1992.

———. *Honour and Shame: The Values of Mediterranean Society*. London: Weidenfeld and Nicholson, 1966.

Philo. Translated by F. H. Colson et al. 10 vols, 2 suppls. Loeb Classical Library. Cambridge: Harvard University Press, 1929–1962.

Pilch, John J. *The Cultural World of Jesus: Sunday by Sunday, Cycle A*. Collegeville, MD: Liturgical, 1995.

Pitt-Rivers, Julian, editor. *Mediterranean Countrymen: Essays in the Social Anthropology of the Mediterranean*. Paris: Mouton, 1963.

———. "Honour and Social Status." In *Honour and Shame: The Values of Mediterranean Society*, edited by J. G. Peristiany, 19–77. Chicago: University of Chicago Press, 1966.

———. *The Fate of Shechem or the Politics of Sex: Essays in the Anthropology of the Mediterranean*. Cambridge: Cambridge University Press, 1977.

Plummer, Alfred. *An Exegetical Commentary on the Gospel According to S. Matthew*. London: Robert Scott, 1928.

Pomeroy, Sarah B. *Goddesses, Whores, Wives, and Slaves: Women in Classical Antiquity*. New York: Schoken, 1975.

Prusher, Ilene R. "As Order Slides, Palestinian Women Face Honor Killings." *Christian Science Monitor* (November 20, 2007) 1.

Qureshi, Tanveer. "The Deadly Ending to a 'Melodrama.'" *The Times (London)*, June 19, 2007, p. 1.

Rabinowitz, J. J. "Marriage Contracts in Ancient Egypt in the Light of Jewish Sources." *Harvard Theological Review* 46 (1953) 91–97.

Raif, Shenai. "Honour-Killing Victim Raped before her Torture Death." *Birmingham Post*, July 20, 2007, p. 2.

Rimmer, Alan. "Honour Killing Riddle of Knifed Girl, 17; Family Quizzed as Pregnant Wife is Found at Home with Multiple Stab Wounds." *Mail on Sunday (London)*, May 13, 2007, p.10.

Robinson, Theodore. *The Gospel of Matthew*. London: Hodder and Stoughton, 1928.

Rohrbaugh, Richard L. "Introduction." In *The Social Sciences and New Testament Interpretation*, edited by Richard L. Rohrbaugh, 1–15. Peabody: Hendrickson, 1996.

Ruggi, Suzanne. "Honor Killings in Palestine: Commodifying Honor in Female Sexuality." *Middle East Report* 28 (1998) 12–15.

Rule, Andrew K. "Born of the Virgin Mary." *Christianity Today* 4 (December 7, 1959) 3–5.

Saadawi, Nawal. *The Hidden Face of Eve*. Translated and edited by Sherif Hetata. London: Zed, 1980.

Sabir, Nadirah Z. "The Adventures of a Muslim Woman in Atlanta." In *Shattering the Stereotypes: Muslim Women Speak Out*, edited by Fawzia Afzal-Khan, 127–141. Northampton: Olive Branch, 2005.

Sahibjam, F. *The Stoning of Soraya*. New York: Arcade, 1994.

Saywell, Shelley, Sonja Smits, and Arsinée Khanjian, producers. *Crimes of Honour*. New York: First Run/Icarus Films, 1998.

Scally, Derek. "Brother Gets Nine-Year Sentence for 'Honour Killing' of Sister." *The Irish Times*, April 14, 2007, p. 9.

Schaberg, Jane. *The Illegitimacy of Jesus: A Feminist Theological Interpretation of the Infancy Narratives*. New York: Harper & Row, 1987.

Schneemelcher, Wilhelm, editor. *New Testament Apocrypha*. Vol. 1, *Gospels and Related Writings*. Rev ed. English translation edited by by R. McL. Wilson. Louisville: Westminster John Knox, 1991.

Schneider, Jane. "Of Vigilance and Virgins: Honor, Shame, and Access to Resources in Mediterranean Societies." *Ethnology* 10 (1971) 1–24.

Schweizer, Eduard. *The Good News According to Matthew*. Translated by David E. Green. London: SPCK, 1980.

Sev'er, A. *A Cross-Cultural Exploration of Wife Abuse: Problems and Prospectus*. Mellen Studies in Sociology. Queenstown: Edwin Mellen, 1997.

Shah, Hassam Qadir. *There is no "Honour" in Killing: Don't Let Them Get Away with Murder*. Lahore: Shirkat Gah, 2002.

Simonetti, Manlio, editor. *Matthew 1–13*. Ancient Christian Commentary on Scripture: New Testament 1a. Downers Grove, IL: InterVarsity, 2001.

Smid, H. R. *Protevangelium Jacobi: A Commentary*. Apocrypha Novi Testamenti 1. Assen: van Gorcum, 1965.

Smith, Lewis. "Muslim Killed Daughter for the 'Dishonour' of Having Boyfriend." *The Times (London)*, September 30, 2003, p. 5.

Smith, Robert H. *Matthew*. Augsburg Commentary on the New Testament. Minneapolis: Augsburg, 1989.

Souad. *Burned Alive: The Shocking, True Story of One Women's Escape from an 'Honour' Killing*. With Marie-Thérèse Cuny. London: Bantam, 2004.

Spivak, Gayatri Chakravorty. "Can the Subaltern Speak?" In *Marxism and the Interpretation of Culture*, edited by Cary Nelson and Lawrence Grossberg, 271–313. Urbana, IL: University of Illinois Press, 1988.

Stanton, Graham, editor. *The Interpretation of Matthew*. Issues in Religion and Theology 3. Philadelphia: Fortress, 1983.

Stendahl, Krister. *"Quis et Unde?* An Analysis of Matthew 1–2." In *The Interpretation of Matthew*, edited by Graham Stanton, 56–66. Issues in Religion and Theology 3. Philadelphia: Fortress, 1983.

Stoil, Rebecca Anna. "Druse Woman Victim of Suspected Honor Killing." *The Jerusalem Post*, May 4, 2006, p. 2.

Strack, Hermann L., and Paul Billerbeck. *Das Evangelium Nach Matthäus Erläutert aus Talmud und Midrasch*. Kommentar zum Neuen Testament aus Talmud und Midrasch. Munich: Oskar Beck, 1922.

Suetonius. Translated by J. C. Rolfe. 2 vols. Cambridge: Harvard University Press, 1914.

Swain, Jon. "My Family Killed My Sister: I Could Be Next." *Sunday Times (London)*, June 17, 2007, p. 10.

Sweet, Louis Matthews. *The Birth and Infancy of Jesus Christ*. Philadelphia: Westminster, 1906.

Tanveer, Khalid. "Honour's Ghastly Tally." *Hobart Mercury (Australia)*, January 4, 2006, p. 17.

Tatum, W. Barnes. "Origins of Jesus Messiah (Matt 1:1, 18a): Matthew's Use of the Infancy Traditions." *Journal of Biblical Literature* 96 (1977) 523–35.

———. *In Quest of Jesus*. New and rev. ed. Nashville: Abingdon, 1999.

Taylor, Jerome. "Love that can be Lethal: Muslim Couples in Fear of 'Honour' Killing." *The Independent (London)*, June 29, 2007.

Taylor, Vincent. *The Historical Evidence for the Virgin Birth*. Oxford: Clarendon, 1920.

Taylor, Walter. "Jesus Within His Social World: Insights from Archaeology, Sociology, and Cultural Anthropology." In *The Quest for Jesus and the Christian Faith*, edited by Frederick J. Gaiser, 49–71. Word and World Supplement Series 3. St. Paul: Word and World, 1997.

Tintori, Karen. *Unto the Daughters: The Legacy of an Honor Killing in a Sicilian-American Family*. New York: St. Martin's, 2007.

Torjesen, Karen Jo. *When Women Were Priests: Women's Leadership In the Early Church & The Scandal of their Subordination in the Rise of Christianity*. New York: HarperSanFrancisco, 1995.

Tosato, Angelo. "Joseph, Being a Just Man (Matt 1:19)." *Catholic Biblical Quarterly* 41 (1979) 547–51.

Triandis, Harry C. "Cross-cultural Studies of Individualism and Collectivism." In *Nebraska Symposium on Motivation, 1989: Cross-cultural Perspectives*, edited by John J. Berman, 41–133. Lincoln, NE: University of Nebraska Press, 1990.

Trilling, Wolfgang. *The Gospel According to St. Matthew*. Vol. 1. London: Burns & Oates, 1969.

Turner, H. E. W. "Expository Problems: The Virgin Birth." *The Expository Times* 68 (1956) 12–17.

Twomey, John. "Mother-In-Law, 70, will Die in Jail for Bride's Honour Killing." *The Express*, September 20, 2007, p. 31.

Bibliography

Van Aarde, Andries G. "The Evangelium infantium, the Abandonment of Children, and the Infancy Narrative in Matthew 1 and 2 from a Social-scientific Perspective." *Society of Biblical Literature Seminary Papers* 31 (1992) 435–53.

Verma, Sonia. "Miss Israel Finalist Quits after Family's Honour Killing Plot." *The Times (London)*, March 9, 2007, p. 35.

Von Campenhausen, Hans. *The Virgin Birth in the Theology of the Ancient Church.* London: SCM, 1964.

Walsh, Declan. "'We Feel No Shame' – The Brothers Who Killed their Sister for Honour: Tragic Tale Highlights Scale of Beatings and Murder of Women in Countryside." *The Guardian (London)*, February 7, 2007, p. 23.

Ward, David. "Sikh Wife's Affair Sparks Honour Killing by Husband and His Mother." *The Guardian (London)*, May 3, 2007, p. 4.

Warnock, Kitty. *Land before Honour: Palestinian Women in the Occupied Territories.* New York: Monthly Review, 1990.

Wells, Bruce. "Sex, Lies, and Virginal Rape: The Slandered Bride and False Accusations in Deuteronomy." *Journal of Biblical Literature* 124 (2005) 41–72.

Weren, Wim J. C. "The Five Women and Matthew's Genealogy." *Catholic Biblical Quarterly* 59 (1997) 288–305.

Westbrook, Raymond. *Old Babylonian Marriage Law.* Horn, Austria: Berger, 1988.

Wharton, Jane. "Stoned to Death as 1,000 Villagers Take Pictures . . . Her Crime? Loving a Man From the Wrong Religion." *The Express.* May 4, 2007, p. 17.

Wikan, Unni. "Shame and Honor: A Contestable Pair." *Man* 19 (1984) 635–52.

———. *In Honor of Fadime: Murder and Shame.* Rev. and ext. ed. Chicago: University of Chicago Press, 2008.

Witherington III, Ben. *Women in the Earliest Churches.* Cambridge: Cambridge University Press, 1988.

"World Diary: Honor Killings." Michael Davie, filmmaker. National Geographic Television, February 13, 2002.

Zervos, G. "Dating the Protevangelium of James: The Justin Martyr Connection." In *Society of Biblical Literature 1994 Seminar Papers*, edited by E. Lovering, 415–34. Atlanta: Scholars, 1994.

Zoepf, Katherine. "25% of Wives in Syria are Abused, UN Study Finds." *The International Herald Tribune*, April 12, 2006, p. 5.